MARGARET SKINNIDER (1893–1971) was born to immigrant Irish parents in Coatbridge, North Lanarkshire. A mathematics teacher, she joined the Glasgow branch of Cumann na mBan in 1915 and became involved in smuggling detonators and bomb-making equipment into Ireland. During the Easter Rising she was a sniper and despatch rider attached to James Connolly's Irish Citizen Army and stayed in Dublin at the home of her mentor, Countess Markievicz, the unofficial headquarters of the rebellion. Shot while setting fire to houses in Harcourt Street, she was taken to hospital where she was interrogated before being released. *Doing My Bit For Ireland* was published in 1917 in New York, where she stayed for some years before returning to Dublin where she resumed teaching and became a leading member of the Irish National School Teachers' Association.

KIRSTY LUSK is a doctoral candidate at the University of Glasgow. She received her MPhil in Irish Writing from Trinity College Dublin and holds an MA (Hons) in English Literature from the University of Glasgow. She is currently researching Scottish-Irish connections in the late 19th and early 20th centuries from a literary perspective in order to explore the legacy of independence, equality and commemoration within a comparative Irish-Scottish framework. She was the co-editor of *Scotland and the Easter Rising* and is currently editing a new edition of Nora Connolly's book, *The Unbroken Tradition*.

Doing My Bit For Ireland

A first-hand account of the Easter Rising

MARGARET SKINNIDER

Luath Press Limited
EDINBURGH
www.luath.co.uk

First published by The Century Co., New York, 1917
New edition 2016

ISBN: 978-1-910745-50-2

The paper used in this book is recyclable. It is made from
low chlorine pulps produced in a low energy, low
emission manner from renewable forests.

Printed and bound by CPI Antony Rowe, Chippenham

Typeset in 11 point Sabon

Typographical arrangement, foreword and timeline
© Luath Press Ltd

All images Wikimedia Commons/National Library of Ireland on
The Commons @ Flickr Commons unless otherwise indicated.

Contents

Map of Dublin	6
Foreword by Kirsty Lusk	9
Timeline	29
Introduction by Margaret Skinnider	39
Chapter 1	43
Chapter 2	55
Chapter 3	67
Chapter 4	73
Chapter 5	83
Chapter 6	97
Chapter 7	107
Chapter 8	115
Chapter 9	121
Chapter 10	127
Chapter 11	135
Chapter 12	143
Chapter 13	149
Suggested Further Reading	174

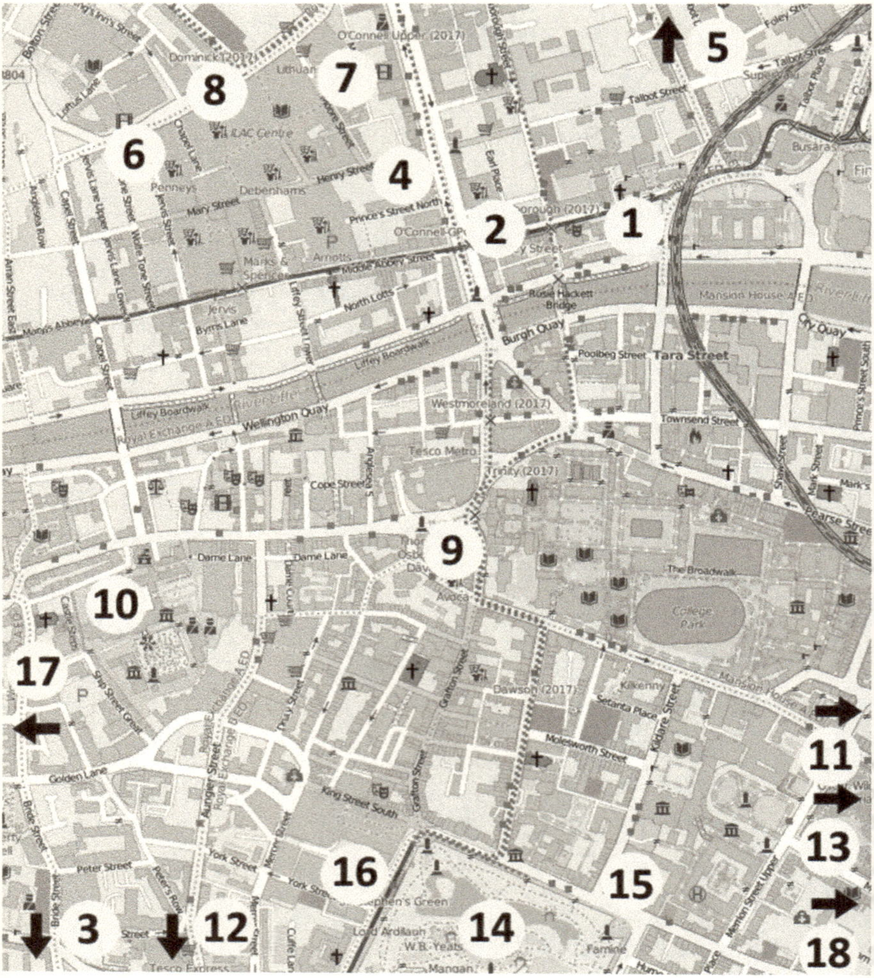
1
2
3
4
5
6
7
8
9
10
11
12
13
14
15
16
17
18
O'Connell Upper (2017)
Dominick (2017)
Foley Street
Talbot Street
Busaras
ILAC Centre
Chapel Lane
Henry Street
Penneys
Debenhams
Mary Street
Prince's Street North
O'Connell GPO
Earl Place
Marks & Spencer
Arnotts
Middle Abbey Street
North Lotts
Jervis
Byrns Lane
Liffey Street Lower
Liffey Boardwalk
Rosie Hackett Bridge
Burgh Quay
Poolbeg Street
Tara Street
Mansion House A ED
City Quay
Westmoreland (2017)
Wellington Quay
Royal Exchange A ED
Townsend Street
Tesco Metro
Trinity (2017)
Cope Street
Pearse Street
Dame Lane
The Broadwalk
Avoca
College Park
Grafton Street
Dawson (2017)
Kilkenny
Setanta Place
Kildare Street
Molesworth Street
Golden Lane
Aungier Street
Royal Exchange B ED
King Street South
Drury Street
Peter Street
York Street
Mercer Street
St Stephen's Green
Lord Ardilaun
W.B. Yeats
Famine
Mangan
Tesco Express
Merrion Street Upper
Bride Street
Peter's Row
Capel Street
Jervis Street
Wolfe Tone Street
Anglesea Row
Loftus Lane
Bolton Street
Arran Street East
Mary's Abbey
Castle Street
Ship Street Great
Shaw Street
Mark Street
Prince's Street South

Key to Map of Dublin

1. 18 Beresford Place (at Eden Quay). Liberty Hall, headquarters of the Irish Citizen Army founded by James Connolly.
2. Sackville Street Lower (now O'Connell Street). The Metropole Hotel, occupied by the Volunteers, was gutted by fire during the Easter Rising.
3. Surrey House at 49b Leinster Road, Rathmines, the home of Countess Markievicz, a role model to Skinnider.
4. The General Post Office (GPO) the rebels' Headquarters where James Connolly commanded military operations.
5. Connolly Station, named in honour of James Connolly.
6. Jervis Street Hospital, where anti-Volunteer forces mounted machine guns on the roof.
7. Moore Street where Charles Carrigan, an Irish Volunteer from Glasgow, was shot dead, leading the charge with The O'Rahilly.
8. Great Britain Street (now Parnell Street). After their surrender, Volunteers were herded into the Rotunda Gardens.
9. College Green. Trinity College Dublin was held by the British during the Rising.
10. Dublin Castle. Sean Connolly was killed leading the Irish Citizen Army's failed attempt to take the Castle, the British administration headquarters.
11. Grand Canal Dock. Boland's Bakery was occupied by the 3rd Battalion of the Volunteers.
12. Harcourt Street Station was occupied by the Volunteers. Skinnider was shot three times attempting to set fire to houses in nearby Harcourt Street.
13. Mount Street Bridge (over Grand Canal). On Wednesday 26 April, much of the fighting took place here.
14. St Stephen's Green, where Skinner and the Volunteers camped before retreating to the Royal College of Surgeons.
15. 27–32 St Stephen's Green. The British mounted a machine gun on the roof of the Shelbourne Hotel.
16. Royal College of Surgeons in Ireland, on St Stephen's Green at York Street, where Margaret Skinnider was based as a despatch rider and sniper during the Easter Rising under the command of Countess Markievicz and Michael Mallin.
17. Kilmainham Gaol, where 14 leaders of the Rebellion were executed by firing squad between 3 and 12 May.
18. St Vincent's Hospital, where Skinnider was treated for pneumonia and gunshot wounds.

Foreword

Kirsty Lusk

THE NAME OF Margaret Skinnider (1892–1971) should be more widely known, and her vital contribution to the struggle for Irish independence more fully acknowledged, both in the centenary year of the Easter Rising and beyond. A 23-year-old schoolteacher from Coatbridge in Scotland, Margaret joined the Irish Citizen Army and fought as a dispatch rider and sniper during Easter Week. She was commended three times for bravery in dispatches to the General Post Office. Her participation was cut short when she was shot three times in the back on Wednesday 26 April 1916. Margaret was the only female combatant to be severely wounded. Her contribution to the events of 1916 did not stop at arming herself and risking her life.

In 1917 Margaret's memoir, *Doing My Bit For Ireland,* was published in New York by Century Company. It was one of the first personal accounts published by a participant and did much to share the rebels' story and encourage American support for the Irish cause. *Doing My Bit For Ireland* is an important perspective on Easter Week and one that provides a fascinating insight into the role of women in 1916. Margaret's writing focuses on the importance and bravery of these female participants, regardless of their role in the conflict, and outlines their professionalism in the face of great risk. Yet she also explains the reasons that they took those risks, and why she did. For Margaret, nationalism, feminism and equal rights for social classes intersected naturally. Margaret saw national self-determination as the method by which to improve social conditions, to do away with the slums of Dublin and improve the lives of children, to bring about equal suffrage and allow women their say in politics. Whether by gun or words, Margaret was committed to an Ireland in which everyone was valued for their contribution, and no one was discriminated against for gender or class. In this respect, it is clear to see why her story is still so relevant today. Inequality was Margaret's most hated enemy, and the one she would fight against her entire life.

Margaret Skinnider was born on 28 May 1892 at 116 Main Street, Coatbridge, to James Skinnider, a stonemason from Tydavnet, County Monaghan, Ireland, and Jane Doud from Barrhead, Renfrewshire. Her parents married on 20 November 1880 in Bothwell and Margaret was brought up with five older siblings Thomas, James, Isabelle, Joseph and Mary, and one younger sister Catherine, who often went by her middle name Georgina. The family travelled to Monaghan every summer for their holidays, Margaret's first introduction to Ireland. By 1901, the Skinniders had moved to 64 St John Street in Maryhill, Glasgow, now known as Barron Street. Margaret followed in her older sister Isabelle's footsteps and trained as a teacher before working at St Agnes' School in Lambhill, Glasgow. She lived at 14 Kersland Street, Hillhead, in Glasgow's West End with the rest of her family, although her older brothers regularly travelled and were often away, including visits to Quebec and New York.

In 1914, Margaret became involved in the suffrage

movement in Scotland and described herself as known to the police as a militant suffragette, of which there were estimated to be around 100 in Scotland. The suffragettes' actions included burning down buildings and pouring acid into letterboxes to destroy the mail. It is a point often raised that 1916 was a violent uprising, but it did not arise out of a vacuum. A culture of arms, violence and war existed across Britain and Ireland in their entirety by 1914 and Margaret's introduction to this came through physical force suffragism in Scotland, not nationalism. On 10 June 1914, Margaret was present at the protests outside Perth Prison against the violent force-feeding of the imprisoned suffragettes who had been on hunger strike. Margaret joined the picket line outside to allow Helen Crawfurd, a Scottish suffragette and communist who supported home rule, to attend the Royal Visit to Perth. Suffragettes would interrupt the visit but according to Helen, Margaret 'had no time for Kings and Queens'.[1]

In 1914 Margaret also joined the Irish Volunteers in Glasgow. The military organisation had been formed in Ireland in 1913 in response to the signing of the Ulster Covenant and the formation of the Ulster Volunteers in 1912. The Ulster Volunteers were organised to stop the implementation of Home Rule for Ireland at any cost; the Irish Volunteers emerged to safeguard Home Rule. A civil war seemed likely. The Home Rule bill was agreed by the House of Commons in 1914 – at the same time as a Home Rule bill for Scotland – but political change was put on hold by the outbreak of the First World War in August 1914. Members of the Irish Volunteers and Ulster Volunteers alike signed up to fight for the British Army. The Irish Volunteers split in September 1914. The majority followed parliamentarian John Redmond, who believed that by proving their loyalty, they would ensure the implementation of Home Rule when the war drew to an end. The reorganisation after the split placed the secretive Irish Republican Brotherhood (IRB), committed to Irish independence, in a stronger position amongst the remaining Irish Volunteers.

In April 1914, *Cumann na mBan* (The Women's Council) was formed. The female paramilitary organisation stated in its constitution that its purpose was to 'advance the cause of Irish liberty and to organise Irishwomen in the furtherance of this object'. The majority of the organisation supported the Irish Volunteers who rejected the call to sign up to the British Army in 1914. When the Anne Devlin branch of *Cumann na mBan* was set up in Glasgow in mid-1915, Margaret Skinnider joined the organisation. In October 1915, Margaret assisted in a raid on Henderson Admiralty Shipyard in Partick, Glasgow, for weapons to send over to Ireland. According to her colleague, Seamus Reader, it was a failed attempt. What they had believed would be a 12-pounder ship's gun turned out to be a fire extinguisher beneath a tarpaulin. Along with other *Cumann na mBan* members, Margaret had been tasked with observing the wall and footpath whilst the Volunteers searched the shipyard.

Skinnider's preparations for the Rising extended beyond acting as a lookout. Margaret learned to shoot in one of the rifle practice clubs in Glasgow, which had been formed to enable women to help in defence of the British Empire in case of invasion. She became an expert shot.

There were tensions over the activities of *Cumann na mBan* however, and the relationship with the men's organisation, the Irish Volunteers. In October 1915, Constance Georgine Markievicz, Countess Markievicz (1868–1927), a suffragette, Irish nationalist, socialist and trade unionist complained that '[t]oday the women attached to the national movements are there chiefly to collect funds for the men to spend'.[2] Markievicz would soon become a powerful role model for Margaret, who shared her strong beliefs and also her wish for active participation in the struggle for Irish independence. At Christmas 1915, Margaret travelled to Dublin to meet with Countess Markievicz for the first time. Margaret crossed the Irish Sea at night, with bomb detonators hidden under her hat, the wires wrapped around her body beneath her coat.

It was an eventful trip. Whilst in Ireland Margaret would test explosives in the Wicklow Hills, practise shooting while disguised as a male member of the boy scout organisation *Na Fianna Éireann*, draw up plans of the Barracks for dynamiting and meet both Thomas MacDonagh and James Connolly.

In January, however, Margaret was forced to return to Glasgow to resume her teaching work in the city. It was a difficult time for her with little information about plans for the Rising reaching Glasgow. Conscription came into force in Scotland in February 1916.

Irish Volunteers called up for the British Army would slip across the Irish Sea and join the garrison at Kimmage, to fight for Ireland when the Rising began. Not all of the West of Scotland Volunteers received as much information however. John Mulholland, Scotland's Representative on the Irish Republican Brotherhood Supreme Council in 1914, and president of the organisation, had voted against staging an uprising before the end of the war, likely for constitutional reasons. Mulholland resigned and left the organisation immediately after explaining his decision to the circles in Glasgow. His replacement as Scottish Representative, Charles Carrigan, would become a member of the Kimmage Garrison after being conscripted and was killed in the Moore Street charge alongside The O'Rahilly. Mulholland's influence would have its effect however. When news of the planned Rising was communicated to Mulholland, he did not inform the executive in Glasgow until Saturday 22 April, stopping the Scottish forces from mobilising in time. Around 56 Scots were members of the Kimmage Garrison during the Rising, but many Irish Volunteers in the West of Scotland would know nothing of the events of Easter Week until they were reported in the Scottish newspapers, by which time it was too late.

For many of the Irish organisations in Ireland, anti-recruitment efforts constituted a major element in their plans. Two hundred thousand Irishmen fought in the First World War and between 30,000 and 49,000 Irishmen were killed.[3] There was a realistic threat of conscription, and economic conscription had already been put into practice. Men were being released from jobs or turned away from work with the intent that they would take up paid employment in the army – known as the 'King's Shilling'. It was a highly effective method in encouraging the lower classes to enlist. It was not the only method at the disposal of the British Government however.

Irish recruitment agents appealed to Irishmen to protect the rights of small nations, a move seen as deeply ironic by many Irish nationalists. James Connolly wrote that:

In India, in Egypt, in Flanders, in Gallipoli, the green
flag is used by our rulers to encourage Irish soldiers
of England to give up their lives for the power that
denies their country the right of nationhood.[4]

The anti-war movement was not just about nationalism. For Connolly, whom Skinnider deeply admired, the First World War was an imperialist and capitalist venture that set the working classes against each other. It had been Connolly's hope that socialists across Europe would come together in rejection of the war, but he was sorely disappointed. Connolly wrote that:

[there were those of] us who believe that the signal
of war ought also to have been the signal for
rebellion, that when the bugles sounded the first
note for actual war, their notes should have been
taken as the tocsin for social revolution.[5]

There would not be the Europe-wide rejection of war that Connolly had hoped for, but he made his opinion clear. From Liberty Hall there hung a sign just prior to the Rising:

WE SERVE NEITHER KING NOR KAISER,
BUT IRELAND

It was as much a rejection of the ongoing war as it was a statement of national self-determination.

The Irish fighting in the British army in this period have remained largely unseen and undiscussed until recent years. These Irish soldiers who fought for the British army would return home to an Ireland 'changed utterly', to a Dublin that had been shelled by the British army they had been fighting for. Two hundred and sixty civilians were killed during Easter Week; many more were injured. In the trenches on the front, the German soldiers held up a sign to the Irish soldiers that stated 'The military are shooting down your wives and children in Dublin.' Those Irish soldiers who had gone out to fight for Ireland – as rebels or members of the British army – would find themselves remembered very differently. In the initial aftermath of Easter Week, however, responses to the actions of the rebels were overwhelmingly negative, likely because so many Irishmen were fighting abroad at the time. It was with the executions of the leaders of 1916, amongst others, and the stories about those who had participated in the Rising, that opinion began to change.

It was for this reason that Margaret would tell her story.

Easter Week 1916

On Holy Thursday, 1916, Margaret Skinnider returned to Dublin and joined the Irish Citizen Army (ICA) in Liberty Hall at the invitation of Countess Markievicz. The ICA was formed of workingmen and women and had been set up in 1913 by James Connolly and Jim Larkin after the atrocities visited on strikers and crowds during the Dublin Lockout. A smaller organisation than the Irish Volunteers, they numbered around 250 and would drill openly in Dublin. The ICA was unique amongst the Irish military organisations of the time in that it allowed women to join and participate to the same extent as men. Countess Markievicz claimed that '[t]here were a considerable number of ICA women. These were absolutely on the same footing as men', and that 'Connolly made it clear to us that unless we women took our share in the drudgery of training and preparing, we should not be allowed to take any share at all in the fight'.[6] It was not the same in other organisations: 'At first, members of *Cumann na mBan* were turned away from many posts, including the GPO. When this news filtered back to the leaders a directive was sent to accept any of the women who wished to take part'.[7] This did not mean that all were in agreement however:

> De Valera refused to have women participate at his outpost. He did not want women who were untrained for soldiering. Afterwards he admitted that he was sorry that he had not used their help, as some of his best men were engaged in cooking rather than fighting.[8]

According to Sinead McCoole, 'Edward Daly was another who only accepted women into his garrison upon receipt of the directive from the GPO'.[9] Even in the GPO there continued to be bias against women: Catherine Rooney (née Byrne) relates in her witness statement how she had to enter the GPO through a window with the aid of two Volunteers after having been refused at the main entrance. Connolly's Irish Citizen Army, however, continued to treat male and female participants equally. For Connolly as for Skinnider, nationalism, feminism and socialism were bound together. It was for this reason that many female participants in Easter Week were members of, or became attached to, the Irish Citizen Army. Amongst their number were Dr Kathleen Clarke, Helena Molony, Elizabeth Farrell and Julia Grenan.

As an ICA member, Skinnider was immediately put to work. Preparations were well under way in Liberty Hall for the Rising, and Citizen Army members surrounded the hall as it had barely avoided a raid thanks to the quick thinking of Connolly and Markievicz. The sense of urgency was heightened by the secret order for the arrest of members of all Irish organisations in Dublin, including the Irish Citizen Army and Irish Volunteers which Connolly showed to Skinnider. After being sent to work making cartridges, Skinnider was given a dispatch to take to Connolly's house in Belfast in the evening. It was here that she met Connolly's daughter, Nora. The two women were of a similar age, both around 23, and went on to become lifelong friends. Mrs Connolly and her daughters returned to Dublin with Skinnider after the dispatch had been delivered. The following days were spent in continued preparation.

The intended date for the start of the Rising was Easter Sunday, 23 April 1916. This was delayed, however, thanks to a demobilisation order for the Irish Volunteers. The order was given by Eoin MacNeill, triggered by the sinking of the *Aud* and the loss of a great number of arms. Though Patrick Pearse challenged the order it had a lasting effect, and the number of combatants was greatly reduced, bringing an end to any potential for an uprising across the whole of Ireland. The Irish Citizen Army in its entirety (219 men and women) alongside the four battalions of Irish Volunteers in Dublin combined to form the first Irish Republican Army. The Rising began on Monday 24 April.

During the Rising, Margaret was attached to the St Stephen's Green garrison, under the command of

Michael Mallin and Countess Markievicz. St Stephen's Green is a public park of 20 acres on the south side of Dublin, roughly a mile from the General Post Office. A major transport hub, it had symbolic as well as militaristic importance. At the north entrance to the park is Fusilier's Arch, erected in 1907 to the war dead, known locally to nationalists in 1916 as 'Traitor's Arch'. Mallin successfully seized Harcourt Street Station, cutting off transport links. Unfortunately, lacking the numbers to take the surrounding buildings as well as the park itself, it was impossible to hold the Green for any length of time, particularly once the army erected a machine gun on the roof of the Shelbourne Hotel.

Margaret worked as a scout and dispatch rider, a dangerous role that took her across Dublin and regularly saw her face machine gun fire. Whilst carrying dispatches, Margaret saw the charge of the 5th Lancers on O'Connell Street and the raising of the Irish flag over the General Post Office. In the early hours of Tuesday, Margaret was sent with a dispatch to the GPO when those encamped in St Stephen's Green were forced to evacuate and retreat to the Royal College of Surgeons by the machine gun fire from the Shelbourne. Margaret had barely returned when she was sent out again to bring in the 16 men guarding the Leeson Street Bridge. Margaret was successful but had to brave the gunfire several times in her continued dispatch work.

The garrison was noted as being particularly well disciplined, despite suffering severely from food shortages. After the portrait of Queen Victoria was slashed, Mallin threatened to shoot anyone who performed similar acts of vandalism and those present assembled at the same time each day for the rosary. By Wednesday there was little in the way of dispatches to be delivered and on the orders of Countess Markievicz, Margaret Skinnider was assigned to the roof of the College of Surgeons to fight as a sniper.

Margaret switched between work as sniper and dispatch rider until late on Wednesday evening, when she concocted a plan to dislodge the soldiers from the roof of the Shelbourne. As Brian Hughes notes, 'while women were placed in harm's way to a greater extent in Mallin's than other garrisons there is still evidence that this was done with some reluctance'.[10] Margaret argued with Mallin to allow her participation in the bombing, using the words of the proclamation against him. Mallin conceded but first assigned Margaret to lead a group of four men to set fire to an antique shop on Harcourt Street, to cut off the British retreat. Councillor William Partridge's rifle discharged when he used it to break the lock on the shop door. The resulting flash drew the attention of the British snipers. Margaret was shot three times in the upper right arm and spine. Fred Ryan was killed.

Partridge succeeded in carrying Margaret back to the Royal College of Surgeons, where she would remain until the surrender on Sunday 30 April. Not only was she at severe risk from her wounds, she began to suffer from pneumonia and the doctor brought in to treat her used too much corrosive sublimate, burning away much of the skin on her back and arm. Thomas O'Donoghue, a fellow member of the ICA, recalled that, having found bagpipes in the College and begun to play, 'a message was sent to him to stop as it was believed that Margaret Skinnider was dying'.[11]

The rebels' chances had taken a turn for the worse. Commandant of the ICA, James Connolly, was shot in the ankle on Thursday morning and a military cordon cut off the garrisons south of the Liffey from the Headquarters at the General Post Office. ICA member Chris Caffrey attempted to cross the cordon dressed in widow's weeds, but was caught and forced to eat her dispatch. When asked what she was chewing, she offered the officer a sweet.

At 3.45pm on Saturday 29 April, Patrick Pearse signed the order for the unconditional surrender of the rebel forces. James Connolly, badly wounded, co-signed the order for the Irish Citizen Army garrisons at Dublin City Hall and St Stephen's Green. General Brigadier Maxwell Lowe accepted the surrender and Nurse Elizabeth O'Farrell, attached to the ICA, was sent across Dublin to each garrison to deliver the orders.

When Elizabeth Farrell arrived at the Royal College of Surgeons, Mallin was asleep and Countess Markievicz took the order to him. Hughes reports that 'after this meeting, the garrisons were assembled and Mallin read out the surrender order, apparently breaking down at least once before regaining his composure.'[12] Mallin did not immediately reply, allowing any soldiers who wished to avoid arrest to leave the garrison. Few did so, despite his orders, 109 men and ten women surrendered. Margaret Skinnider was transferred to St Vincent's Hospital, with Countess Markievicz's will hidden in the lining of her coat. It was the last time that she would see Michael Mallin, who was executed on 8 May 1916 at Kilmainham Gaol.

After the Rising

Margaret remained in St Vincent's Hospital until 27 May 1916, the day before her 24th birthday. She narrowly avoided arrest thanks to the head doctor at St Vincent's, who demanded her release from Bridewell Prison after she was taken there, insisting that she was not well enough to begin a prison sentence. It was in hospital that she learned of the executions of the Rising leaders, many of whom she had known personally. After her release, she applied for a permit from Dublin Castle to return to Glasgow. It was a risk but she was successful, owing in part to her '"loyal" Scotch accent'.[13]

On her return Skinnider could not resume teaching, as she was still unable to use her right arm. Instead, over the summer she travelled to England to visit the Volunteers incarcerated in Reading Jail. In July and August of 1916, Nora Connolly stayed with Skinnider in Glasgow. Skinnider assisted Connolly in procuring a passport to America by providing her Glasgow address. At the same time, Skinnider returned again briefly to Dublin before she travelled to New York to visit her brother Thomas and to share the story of Easter Week.[14] Skinnider travelled on the Clydebuilt steamer, *California*, arriving on 11 December 1916.[15] In New York, Margaret lived with Nora Connolly and wrote her autobiographical account of Easter Week. In a review published in *The Dial* newspaper in 1917, the anonymous reviewer wrote:

> One of the chief virtues of Miss Skinnider's simple recital is that it makes the Irish revolutionists live for us, especially their executed leaders, so that the Irish question presents itself as an essentially human problem, and the right of small nations changes from a battle cry to a demand for constructive thought.[16]

Margaret Skinnider was forced to return to Glasgow in 1918 because of visa problems, remaining in the city for several months before moving to Dublin in 1919.[17] There, she worked for the Irish Transport and General Worker's Union, remaining active in *Cumann na mBan* during the Irish War of Independence (1919–21), training Volunteers amongst other duties. During this time, Margaret went through great personal loss. Her father died on 17 October 1917 in Glasgow. Her mother was killed when her ship, the ss *Rowan*, sank on 9 October 1921. Jane Skinnider had been travelling back from Dublin after visiting Margaret there.

With the agreement of the Anglo-Irish Treaty and the outbreak of the Civil War, Skinnider became a member of the Anti-Treaty forces. After the battle of the Four Courts, she became IRA paymaster general until her arrest in 1922 for possession of a revolver and ammunition. Skinnider spent 11 months in Mountjoy prison and was released in 1923. By 1925, Skinnider was working as a clerk at the Workers' Union of Ireland and was Chief Officer of *Cumann na mBan*. At this time, she applied for a military pension and was refused on the grounds that she was not a soldier in 'the masculine sense'.[18] She would not receive her pension until 1938.

Around 1928, Skinnider was finally able to return to teaching and gained a position at Irish Sisters of Charity national school, Kings Inns Street, Dublin, where she would remain until her retirement. Skinnider was described as an excellent teacher by her pupils, strict but fair. She taught the students who were to go on to high school and also coached the camogie team. Class sizes at the time were around 60 but Margaret's classes were well disciplined. On Friday afternoons, she would roll down the blinds and her classes would sing rebel songs. The blinds were closed because the other teachers – primarily nuns – did not approve. Margaret was not fond of some of the approaches taken by her colleagues to teaching but also believed that education began in the home. One student, Maureen, described how, after her brother had been killed in an accident, Miss Skinnider took flowers to the house in North Dublin.

During this period, Skinnider became increasingly involved in the Irish National Teachers' Organisation (INTO) and campaigned for equal pay, pensions, training and status for all teachers, participating in the six-month long strike in 1946. From 1949 until 1961, she served as a central executive committee member of INTO and in 1950 she ran in local council elections as a candidate for *Clann na Poblachta* but was unsuccessful.[19] Skinnider was elected to the national executive of *Clann na Poblachta* in May 1953.[20] She became Vice-President of INTO (1955–56) and President (1956–57), concentrating on parity of salary with secondary teachers, pensions and teacher training.[21] Skinnider regularly stated that 'cooperation by parents is the greatest single factor in education'.[22] In 1957, Skinnider ran as a candidate in the Senate General Election for the Labour panel.[23]

As President of INTO, Skinnider represented Ireland at the 34-Nation conference of the World Confederation of Organisations of the Teaching Professions, where she declared: 'When you have understanding amongst nations, you have peace.'[24] Her ship, the ss *Ascanius*, returned via Singapore, Penang, Colombo, Port Said, Marseille and Liverpool.

After her retirement, Skinnider remained engaged with improving teachers' rights and served on the Irish Congress of Trade Unions executive council from 1961 until 1963. She also wrote to *The Irish Times* in 1964 to protest at the low pension rates, signing the note 'Margaret Skinnider, ICA, 1916'.[25] She remained unmarried and died on 10 October 1971. Margaret Skinnider was buried in the Republican plot in Glasnevin Cemetery, Dublin.

Doing Her Bit For Ireland (and Scotland)

Margaret Skinnider wrote her account of the Rising to educate and inform an international audience about the Easter Rising in Dublin. Retrospectively, her account has provided insight into the three main movements behind the Rising: nationalism, feminism and labour rights. She has given voice to repressed elements of the Rising, particularly militant feminism. Not only an engaging story, Margaret's memoir draws attention to Irish-Scottish connections, to cross border concerns such as labour and the suffrage movement and to the militancy that already existed in the United Kingdom and prepared the ground for the Rising.

In comparisons between Irish and Scottish Independence movements, the difference has often been defined as a violent versus a peaceful revolution. Such a contrast does not take into account the hundred years that has passed since. Margaret's revolutionary tendencies did not just come from her involvement in the Irish Volunteers, it was Scotland that gave her the tools to take to Ireland – whether through the rifle club set up in defence of the British Empire at which she trained or through her role as a militant suffragette. Those she admired most, such as James Connolly and Michael Mallin, had served in the British Army, and their own revolutionary mind-sets had been formed whilst in those ranks. The First World War recruiters spoke of using violence to defend the rights of small nations. In many aspects, the Easter Rising was a product of its time and the militarism that Britain and Ireland were engulfed in. This is something that Margaret makes very clear throughout *Doing My Bit For Ireland*. She also argues that independence goes beyond national self-determination and requires equal rights to be truly effective.

Perhaps what Margaret's account makes most clear is just how far there is still to go in terms of equal rights, whether through gender equality or class equality or human rights. *Doing My Bit For Ireland* raises the questions of how much has changed in a hundred years, and how much still has to change. It is also a reminder of how similar Ireland and Scotland are; of the issues that cross borders, issues of war and peace, equality and justice, repression and resistance. It is a story to analyse, argue and engage with, and above all a story to learn from and listen to with care.

Margaret Skinnider's story is never stronger or more important than when she tells it herself.

Endnotes

1. Marx Memorial Library, London, *Memoirs of Helen Crawfurd*, p.106.
2. Markievicz, Countess Constance, 'Buy a Revolver' in *In Their Own Voice: Women and Irish Nationalism* (1995) ed. Margaret Ward (Cork: Attic Press, 2001) pp.51-53.
3. There is a discrepancy over exact numbers. 30,000 Irishmen were killed from Irish regiments however it is suspected that the realistic death toll when including Irishmen who joined other regiments was closer to 49,000.
4. Connolly James, 'The Irish Flag' in *Worker's Republic* (Dublin, 8 April 1916).
5. Connolly James, 'Revolutionary Unionism and War' in *International Socialist Review* (March 1915).
6. Markievicz, Constance 'Stephen's Green' (1926) in *In Their Own Voices: Women and Irish Nationalism (1995)*, ed. Margaret Ward (Cork: Attic Press, 2001) pp. 73–76, p.73.
7. Sinead McCoole, *No Ordinary Women: Irish Female Activists in the Revolutionary Years, 1900–1923* (Dublin: The O'Brien Press, 2003) p.39.
8. Ibid. p.38.
9. Ibid. p.60.
10. Hughes, Brian, *16 Lives: Michael Mallin* (Dublin: The O'Brien Press, 2012) p.156.
11. O'Donoghue, Thomas, 'BMH WS 1666' in *Bureau of Military History Archives*.
12. Hughes Brian, *16 Lives: Michael Mallin* (Dublin: The O'Brien Press, 2012) p. 159.
13. Skinnider, Margaret, *Doing My Bit For Ireland* (New York: Century Company, 1917) p. 194.

14 Bureau of Military History Archives, Frank Robbins, *Witness Statement 585*, (1951) p. 113.
15 National Archives at Washington, D.C., Records of the Immigration and Naturalisations Services, *Passenger and Crew Lists of Vessels Arriving at New York, New York, 1897–1957, Ship:* California, *Arrival Date: 11th Dec 1916*.
16 'Doing My Bit For Ireland. By Margaret Skinnider' in *The Dial*, Vol. LXIII, June-December 1917 (Chicago: The Dial Publishing Company) p. 218.
17 See Lusk, Kirsty 'Labour Lives No.18: Margaret Skinnider' in *Saothar*, 41 (Dublin: 2016) pp. 111–113 in which some elements of this section have been previously printed.
18 Military Service Pensions Collection, MSP34REF19910: *Margaret Skinnider*, 1P724, p. 24.
19 *The Irish Times*, Newspaper Archive, '131 Nominations for Dublin Corporation', 9 September 1950, p. 9.
20 *The Irish Times,* Newspaper Archive, 'National Executive of Clann na Poblachta', 26 May 1953, p. 4.
21 *The Irish Times*, Newspaper Archive, 'INTO repeats demand for wage parity', 6 April 1956, p. 4.
22 *The Irish Times*, Newspaper Archive, '10% of primary school pupils are backward – INTO president', 12 December 1956, p. 9.
23 *The Irish Times*, Newspaper Archive, '33 Senators Elected', 11 May 1957, p. 9.
24 *The Irish Times*, Newspaper Archive, 'Irish Teacher at Manila Conference', 9 August 1956, p. 7.
25 *The Irish Times*, Newspaper Archives, 'Pensioner's Pittance', 20 April 1964, p.9.

Timeline

1845–9   Potato blight causes famine in Ireland and prompts mass emigration around the world. Between 1841 and 1851, the Irish population of Scotland increases by 90 per cent with an influx of over 80,000 Irish people.

1868   June – James Connolly born to Irish parents in Edinburgh.

1880   20 November – Skinnider's father and mother, James Skinnider of County Monaghan and Jane Doud of Barrhead, marry in Bothwell.

1882   James Connolly joins the British army, lying about his age. He deserts in 1889.

1889   July – Charles Stewart Parnell makes his first political visit to Scotland and is made a Freeman of Edinburgh. Parnell makes a public speech on Calton Hill.

1891   October – Constitutional nationalism suffers a severe setback with the death of Charles Stewart Parnell.

1892   28 May – Margaret Skinnider born in Coatbridge, Scotland.
         November – James Connolly joins Scottish Labour Party.

1893   Nora Connolly, second child to James and

Lillie Connolly, born in Edinburgh.

1895　First Gaelic League branch outside Ireland formed in Glasgow (the Pádraig Pearse branch remains active in 2016).

1896　May – James Connolly moves to Dublin with his wife Lillie and takes a job as a secretary of the Dublin Socialist Club.

1901　The Skinnider family are staying at 64 St John Street (now Barron Street), Maryhill, Glasgow.

1902　June – Pádraig Pearse visits Glasgow to give an Irish language lecture on 8 June. It is his second visit to the city, the first being in 1899.

1904　Sean MacDiarmada, one of the seven signatories of the Proclamation of the Irish Republic, moves to Edinburgh for work. He returns to Ireland before the end of the year. MacDiarmada goes on to become the contact point for Glasgow Volunteers prior to the Rising.

1905　November – Nationalist Party *Sinn Féin* (We Ourselves) established.

1912　April – Third Home Rule Bill, to establish an Irish parliament to deal with Irish affairs, introduced to Parliament. The bill is due to come into effect in 1914.
September – Over 500,000 Irish Ulster Unionists sign the Ulster Covenant pledging to block any attempts to implement Home Rule.

TIMELINE

1913   January – Ulster Volunteer Force (UVF) established to prevent the introduction of Home Rule.
August – Organised by Jim Larkin, founder of the Irish Transport and General Workers' Union (ITGWU), and James Connolly, thousands of workers across Dublin go on strike for improved conditions and better pay. This event, known as the Dublin Lockout, lasts five months until January 1914.
November – Connolly, along with Jack White and Jim Larkin, establishes the Irish Citizen Army (ICA) to protect striking workers.
December – The Irish Volunteers formed in response to the UVF in order to protect the Irish people.

1914   Skinnider joins the Irish Volunteers in Glasgow. She also joins a local rifle club to learn to shoot.
April – *Cumann na nBan* (the Women's Council) founded as a volunteer force for women to work with the Irish Volunteers.
10 July – Skinnider attends protests in support of suffragettes held in Perth prison. She meets Helen Crawfurd, a Scottish suffragette and communist, and takes her place in the picket to allow her to see the Royal visit.
July – 900 rifles are landed at Howth by the *Asgard*. Nora and Ina Connolly participate in their dispersal. Later that day, the King's Own Scottish Borderers shoot four civilians on Bachelor's Walk, Dublin.
August – Britain declares war on Germany. Scotland sends 690,000 men to the front.

Home Rule Bill postponed for the duration of World War I.

1915 February – Scottish politician, John Campbell Hamilton-Gordon, first Marquess of Aberdeen and Temair, resigns from his second term as Lord Lieutenant of Ireland.
May–September – The Anne Devlin Branch of *Cumann na mBan* formed in Glasgow. Skinnider joins them.
May–September – Irish Republican Brotherhood (IRB), founded in 1858 to fight for Irish Independence, establish a military council. Believing with the outbreak of war that 'England's difficulty is Ireland's opportunity', they begin planning a Rebellion.
October – Irish Volunteers and *Cumann na mBan* members raid Henderson's Admiralty Shipyard in Partick for weapons. Skinnider acts as lookout.
December – Having joined the recently formed Glasgow branch of *Cumann na mBan*, Skinnider travels to Ireland smuggling bomb-making equipment under her hat. Irish Volunteers from Glasgow are regularly smuggling weapons and explosives to Countess Markievicz and Sean MacDiarmada in preparation for action.

1916 January – James Connolly joins IRB military council, adding the forces of the ICA to the planned Easter Rising.
Skinnider returns to Glasgow and resumes teaching.
February – Conscription introduced in Scot-

TIMELINE

land. When members of the Glasgow Irish Volunteers are conscripted, they travel instead to Ireland and join the Kimmage Garrison.

18 April – Pádraig Pearse visits the Kimmage Camp to give talk to Volunteers including the Glasgow participants in the Rising. The Kimmage Garrison is 56-strong.

20 April – (Holy Thursday) Skinnider arrives in Dublin where she joins the Irish Citizen Army. She is sent from Liberty Hall to the Connolly house in Belfast with a message and returns the next day.

21 April – The *Aud* arrives at Tralee Bay carrying 20,000 German rifles for the rebellion but goes unmet by leaders of the Rising.

22 April – The *Aud* captured by British forces. Sir Roger Casement arrested. Eoin MacNeill, commander-in-chief of the Irish Volunteers, issues call to forces not go out on Easter Sunday as planned.

23 April (Easter Sunday) – Meeting of the Military Council to discuss the situation. The Rising put on hold until the following day.

24 April (Easter Monday) – The Rising begins at noon. James Connolly commands military operations from the Headquarters at the General Post Office (GPO) throughout the week. A skilled markswoman, Skinnider takes position as a despatch rider and sniper at the Royal College of Surgeons on St Stephen's Green.

26 April – Skinnider is shot three times attempting to set fire to houses in the nearby Harcourt Street.

27 April – Connolly severely wounded.

28 April – Charles Carrigan, an Irish Volunteer from Glasgow, shot in Moore Street leading the charge with The O'Rahilly. It is his 34th birthday.

29 April – Leaders surrender to British army. Countess Markievicz passes her will to Skinnider who, despite being gravely injured, hides it in the lining of her coat. Skinnider is taken to St Vincent's Hospital where she is questioned by police. Released on medical grounds on 27 May, she gains a permit to return to Scotland.

May – Leaders of the Rebellion are executed by firing squad at Kilmainham Gaol over a nine day period. James Connolly, due to his injuries, has to be tied to a chair for his execution on 12 May. He is the last leader to be executed by firing squad.

27 May – Skinnider released from hospital the day before her 24th birthday.

June – James Connolly's older brother, John, dies in Edinburgh and is buried with full British military honours.

July–August – Nora Connolly stays with Skinnider in Glasgow; using that address, lies about her name to procure a visa to travel to America.

August – Sir Roger Casement executed in London for treason. Sir Arthur Conan Doyle is amongst those who plead for clemency on his behalf.

August – 200 Irish revolutionaries brought to Barlinnie Prison in Glasgow where they remain for only a short period of time before being moved to Frongoch in Wales. Part of the

reason is the sympathy shown to them by the Irish community and Scottish suffragettes.
11 December – Skinnider travels on the SS *California* to New York, where her elder brother lives, joining Nora Connolly there.

1917 Skinnider tours America speaking about the Rising and gathering support for the Republican cause. Her autobiography, *Doing My Bit For Ireland*, published in New York.

1918 Skinnider forced to return to Glasgow because of visa problems.
November – End of World War 1.
December – *Sinn Féin* wins landslide victory in Westminster elections. Members do not take up seats in Parliament. Countess Constance Markievicz is elected first ever female MP.

1919 Skinnider moves permanently to Dublin.
January – *Sinn Féin* establish an Irish government (*Dáil Eireann*) in Dublin. Two days later an isolated attack on a member of the armed police force, the Royal Irish Constabulary (RIC), sparks a series of violent events and guerrilla warfare which lasts three years, known as the Irish War of Independence. Skinnider active in the War, particularly 1920–21.

1921 July – Ceasefire declared.
December – After weeks of talks and negotiations, Anglo-Irish Treaty signed by Michael Collins and Arthur Griffith. It allows for the

establishment of an Irish Free State, although the King to remain Head of State. It also firmly establishes the border between Northern and Southern Ireland. Opinion polarised in Ireland.

1922　　June – Due to fierce opposition to the terms of the Treaty, civil war erupts in Ireland. During this time, Skinnider works as Paymaster General for the Provisional Irish Republican Army until her arrest on 26 December and subsequent imprisonment for possession of a revolver. Nora Connolly, James Connolly's daughter, takes over Skinnider's position as Paymaster General until her arrest in 1923.
December – Southern Ireland becomes the Irish Free State.

1923　　May – Civil war ends as Anti-Treaty forces are significantly diminished. Skinnider released from prison.

1925　　Skinnider works as a clerk for the Workers' Union of Ireland and is Chief Officer of *Cumann na mBan*. Her application for a Military Service Pension refused on the grounds that she is not 'a soldier in the masculine sense'.

1928　　Skinnider, finally allowed to return to teaching, works at Irish Sisters of Charity National School, Kings Inns Street, Dublin, where she remains until her retirement. She teaches the eldest primary students, preparing them for high school; she also takes the school camogie team.

TIMELINE

1938   Skinnider receives her military pension, 13 years after she first applied.

1946   The Irish National Teachers' Organisation (INTO), of which Skinnider is a member, holds a six-month strike for equal pay. High school students used by the government to deal with the shortage of primary school teachers include some of Skinnider's former pupils, aged as young as 14.

1949   Skinnider serves on the INTO Executive Council and continues to do so until 1961.
April – As the Republic of Ireland Act 1948 comes in to effect, Ireland becomes a fully independent nation.

1955–56   Margaret serves as Vice-President of INTO.

1956–57   Elected as President of INTO, Skinnider travels to Manila, the Philippines, to represent Ireland at the world conference of the Organisation of the Teaching Profession.

1961–63   Skinnider retires in 1961 but serves on the Irish Congress of Trade Unions executive council from 1961 to 1963.

1968   June – Plaque to commemorate James Connolly's birthplace is erected in the Cowgate, Edinburgh.

1971   10 October – Skinnider dies in Dublin. She is buried beside famous revolutionary Countess

Markievicz in Glasnevin cemetery, Dublin.

1999　12 May – First meeting of the devolved Scottish Parliament.
December – After years of unrest and violence in Northern Ireland, the Good Friday Agreement signals a degree of peace in the North.

2014　September – Scotland holds referendum on Independence, which is rejected 55 per cent to 45 per cent.

2016　April – Centenary of the Easter Rising. Skinnider's *Doing My Bit For Ireland* republished in her native Scotland. A plaque commemorating her is put up in Coatbridge.

Introduction

WHEN THE REVOLT of a people that feels itself oppressed is successful, it is written down in history as a revolution – as in this country[1] in 1776. When it fails, it is called an insurrection – as in Ireland in 1916. Those who conquer usually write the history of the conquest. For that reason the story of the 'Dublin Insurrection' may become legendary in Ireland, where it passes from mouth to mouth, and may remain quite unknown throughout the rest of the world, unless those of us who were in it and yet escaped execution, imprisonment, or deportation, write truthfully of our personal part in the Rising of Easter week.

It was in my own right name that I applied for a passport to come to this country. When it was granted me after a long delay I wondered if, after all, the English authorities had known nothing of my activity in the Rising. But that can hardly be, for it was a Government detective who came to arrest me at the hospital in Dublin where I was recovering from wounds received during the fighting.

I was not allowed to stay in prison; the surgeon in charge of the hospital insisted to the authorities at Dublin Castle that I was in no condition to be locked up

---

1. The United States of America.

in a cell. But later they might have arrested me, for I was in Dublin twice, once in August and again in November. On both occasions detectives were following me. I have heard that three days after I openly left my home in Glasgow to come to this country inquiries were made for me of my family and friends.

That there is some risk in publishing my story, I am well aware; but that is the sort of risk which we who love Ireland must run, if we are to bring to the knowledge of the world the truth of that heroic attempt last spring to free Ireland and win for her a place as a small but independent nation, entitled to the respect of all who love liberty. It is to win that respect, even though we failed to gain our freedom, that I tell what I know of the Rising.

I find that here in America it is hard to imagine a successful Irish revolt, but there was more than a fighting chance for us as our plans were laid. Ireland can easily be defended by the population once they are aroused, for the country is well suited to guerrilla warfare, and the mountains near the coast form a natural defence from attack by sea. Nor do the people have to go outside for their food. They could easily live for years in the interior on what the soil is capable of producing. And there is plenty of ammunition in Ireland, too. If we had been able to take the British as completely off guard in the country districts as we did in Dublin – had there not been the delay of a day in carrying out concerted action – we could have seized all the arms and ammunition of the British arsenals on the island.

Today it would be harder, for the British are not likely to be again caught unaware of our plans. Besides, they are taking precautions. Drilling of any sort is forbidden; football games are not allowed; all excursions are prohibited. The people are not allowed to come together in numbers on any occasion.

For a long time after the Rising, I dreamed every night about it. The dream was not as it actually took place, for the streets were different and the strategic plans changed, while the outcome was always successful. My awakening was a bitter disappointment, yet the memory of our failure is a greater memory than many of us ever dared to hope.

In all the literature of the Celtic revival through which Ireland has gained fresh recognition from the world there is no finer passage nor one that can mean so much to us than that paragraph of the last proclamation which Pádraig Pearse wrote in the ruined Dublin Post Office when under shell and shrapnel fire. At a moment when he knew that the Rising had been defeated, that the end of his supreme attempt had come, he wrote:

> For four days they (the men) have fought and toiled, almost without cessation, almost without sleep; and in the intervals of fighting, they have sung songs of the freedom of Ireland. No man has complained, no man has asked why? Each individual has spent himself, happy to pour out his strength for Ireland and for freedom. If they do not win this fight, they will at least have deserved to win it. But win it they will, although they may win it in death. Already they have won a great thing. They have redeemed Dublin from many shames, and made her name splendid among the names of cities.

I

JUST BEFORE CHRISTMAS a year ago, I accepted an invitation to visit some friends in the north of Ireland where, as a little girl, I had spent many mid-summer vacations. My father and mother are Irish, but have lived almost all their lives in Scotland and much of that time in Glasgow. Scotland is my home, but Ireland my country.

On those vacation visits to County Monaghan, Ulster, I had come to know the beauty of the inland country, for I stayed nine miles from the town of Monaghan. We used to go there in a jaunting car and on the way passed the fine places of the rich English people – the 'Planter' people we called them because they were of the stock that Cromwell brought over from England and planted on Irish soil. We would pass, too, the small and poor homes of the Irish, with their wee bit of ground. It was then I began to feel resentment, though I was only a child.

In Scotland there were no such contrasts for me to see, but there were the histories of Ireland – not those the English have written but those read by all the young Irish today after they finish studying the Anglicised histories used in the schools. I did it the other way about, for I was not more than 12 when a boyfriend loaned me a big thick book, printed in very small type, an Irish history of Ireland. Later I read the school histories and the resentment I had felt in County Monaghan grew hotter.

Then there were the old poems which we all learned. My favourite was, 'The Jackets Green', the song of a young girl whose lover died for Ireland in the time of William III. The red coat and the green jacket! All the differences between the British and Irish lay in the contrast between those two colours. William III, too! Up to his reign the Irish army had been a reality; Ireland had had a population of nine millions. Today there are only four million Irish in Ireland, a country that could easily support five times that number in ease and comfort. The history of my country after the time of William III seemed to me to be a history of oppression which we should tell with tears if we did not tell it with anger.

But I believed the time was at hand to do something. We all believed that; for an English war is always the signal for an Irish Rising. Ever since this war began, I had been hearing of vague plans. In Glasgow I belonged to the Irish Volunteers and to the *Cumann na mBan*, an organisation of Irish girls and women. I had learned to shoot in one of the rifle practice clubs which the British organised so that women could help in the defence of the Empire.

These clubs had sprung up like mushrooms and died as quickly, but I kept on till I was a good marksman. I believed the opportunity would soon come to defend my own country. And now I was going over at Christmas to learn what hope there was of a rising in the spring.

After all, I did not go to the quiet hills of Monaghan,

but to Dublin at the invitation of the most patriotic and revolutionary woman in all Ireland. Constance Gore-Booth, who by her marriage with a member of the Polish nobility became the Countess Markievicz, had heard of my work in the *Cumman na mBan* and wanted to talk with me. She knew where all the men and women who loved Ireland were working, and sooner or later met them all in spite of the fact that she was of Planter stock and by birth of the English nobility in Ireland.

It was at night that I crossed the Irish Sea. All other passengers went to their staterooms, but I stayed on deck. Leaning back in a steamer chair, with my hat for a pillow, I dropped asleep. That I ever awakened was a miracle. In my hat I was carrying to Ireland detonators for bombs, and the wires were wrapped around me under my coat. That was why I had not wanted to go to a stateroom where I might run into a hot water pipe or an electric wire that would set them off. But pressure, they told me when I reached Dublin, is just as dangerous, and my head had been resting heavily on them all night!

It is hard now to think of that hospitable house in Leinster Road with all the life gone out of it and its mistress in an English prison. Everyone coming to Dublin who was interested in plays, painting, the Gaelic language, suffrage, labour or Irish Nationalism visited there. The Countess Markievicz kept 'open house' not only for her friends, but for her friends' friends. As one of them has written: 'Until she came down to breakfast in the morning, she never knew what guests she had under her roof. In order not to disturb her, they often climbed in through the window late at night.'

The place was full of books; you could not walk about without stumbling over them. There were times, too, when the house looked like the wardrobe in a theatre. You would meet people coming downstairs in all manner of costume for their part in plays the count wrote and 'Madam' – as we called her – acted with the help of whoever were her guests. These theatrical costumes were sometimes used for plays put on at the Abbey Theatre, nearby. They served, too, as disguises for suffragettes or labour leaders wanted by the police; the house was always watched whenever there was any sort of agitation in Dublin.

I remember hearing of one labour leader whom the police hoped to arrest before he could address a mass meeting. He was known to visit Madam, so the plain-clothes men made for Surrey House at once. When they arrived they found a fancy dress ball going on to welcome the count back from Poland. All windows were lighted, music for dancing could be heard, and guests in carriages and motors were arriving. This was no likely haunt for a labour agitator, so they went away. But caution brought them back the next morning, for rumour still had it that their man was hiding there. They waited about the house all that morning and afternoon.

Many persons came and went, among them an old man who walked with difficulty and leaned upon the arm of a young woman. The police paid no more attention to him than to the others, but it was the labour leader in one of the disguises from the theatrical wardrobe.

He made his speech that night surrounded by such a crowd of loyal defenders that he could not be arrested.

During the Transport Workers' strike in 1913, Madam threw open her house as a place of refuge where strikers were sure to find something to eat or a spot to sleep, if only on the drawing room floor. In addition, she sold her jewels to obtain money to establish soup kitchens for their families. Her energy and courage always led her where the conflict was hottest I do not think she knew what it was to be afraid, once she decided upon a course of action. Although belonging to the most privileged class in Ireland by birth and education, as a little girl she had thrown herself into the Irish cause. She and her sister Eva used to go to the stables, take horses without permission, and ride at a mad pace to the big meetings. There they would hear the great Parnell or the eloquent Michael Davitt tell the story of the wrongs done to Ireland, and urge upon their hearers great courage and self-sacrifice that these wrongs might be righted. If all those at such meetings had heeded the speakers' words as did this little daughter of Lady Gore-Booth; had they surrendered themselves as completely as she did, I verily believe we would today be far along the road toward a free Ireland.

As a child, all the villagers on her father's estate loved Madam, for they felt her sincerity. When she was sent away to school or went to Paris to study painting, for which she had marked talent, they missed her. It was while she was in Paris that she met and married another artist, a member of the Polish nobility. Poland and Ireland! Two countries which have had their great history and their great humiliation, now have their hope of freedom!

Neither the count nor countess were willing to permanently give up their country of birth, so they decided to live part of the time in Dublin and part of the time on his estates near Warsaw. It was while Madam was in Poland that she learned some of the fine old Polish airs to which she later put words for the Irish. Upon her return to Ireland she was at last expected to take her place as a social leader in the Dublin Castle set. Instead, she went more ardently than ever into all the different movements that were working towards the freedom of Ireland.

About this time Baden-Powell was organising his British Boy Scouts in Ireland. He was so much impressed with the success that Pádraig Pearse was having with Irish boys that he asked him to help him in the Boy Scout movement. Pearse did not care to make potential British soldiers out of Irish boys, however, and refused this invitation. The incident stirred Madam to urge an Irish Boy Scout movement. She could not find anyone to take it up with energy, so she decided to do it herself with Pearse's cooperation. Madam had never done work of this sort, but that did not deter her. Since it must be an organisation that would do something for Irish spirit in Irish boys, she named it after the *Fianna Éireann*, a military organisation during the reign of Cormac MacAirt, one of the old Irish heroes. Its story was one of daring and chivalry such as would appeal to boys. With this name went instruction in Ireland's history in the days of her independence and great deeds, as well as instruction in scouting and shooting.

At Cullenswood House, where Pádraig Pearse had his boys' school until it outgrew these quarters, there is a fresco in the hall that pictures an old Druid warning the boy hero, Cúchulainn, that whoever takes up arms on a certain day will become famous, but will die an early death. The answer, which became a motto for the boys in that school and also a prophecy of their teacher's death, is in old Irish beneath the fresco, 'I care not if my life has only the span of a night and a day if my deeds be spoken of by the men of Ireland!'

It was in this spirit of devotion to Ireland that the *Fianna* boys were drilled. The house in Leinster Road was always running over with them, some as young as ten years. You would find them studying hard or, just as likely, sliding down the fine old banisters. Madam never went anywhere that they did not follow as a bodyguard. They loved her and trusted her, a high compliment, since I have always found that boys are keen judges of sincerity. If her work had been either pose or mere hysterical enthusiasm, as some English 'friends' in Dublin have sought to make the world believe, these boys would have discovered it quickly enough. As it was, they remained her friends, and two of the younger men, executed after Easter Week, were volunteer officers who received their first training under Madam in the *Fianna*.

The countess was one of the best shots in Ireland, and taught the boys how to shoot. After the Rising, when we all had surrendered, there still was one house from which constant and effective firing went on for three days. At last, a considerable force of British took it by storm. Imagine the surprise of the officer in command when he found that its only occupants were three boys, all under 16!

'Who taught you to shoot like that?' he asked them.

'The Countess Markievicz,' came the answer.

'How often did she drill you?'

'Only on Sundays!' was the reply.

'And these great lumps of mine,' exclaimed the officer in disgust, 'are drilled twice a day and don't yet know their left foot from their right!'

Madam also took real interest in the personal problems of her boys. While I was staying with her at Christmas, she was teaching a boy to sing. He was slowly growing blind, and nothing could be done to save his sight, but she determined that he should have a livelihood, and spent hours of her crowded days in teaching him the words and music of all the best patriotic songs and ballads. If she heard that any of the boys were sick, she would have them brought over to Surrey House where she herself could nurse and cheer them. Between times she would rouse their love of country to a desire to study its history.

When I told Madam I could pass as a boy, even if it came to wrestling or whistling, she tried me out by putting me into a boy's suit, a *Fianna* uniform. She placed me under the care of one of her boys to whom she explained I was a girl, but that, since it might be necessary someday to disguise me as a boy, she wanted to find whether I could escape detection. I was supposed to be one of the Glasgow *Fianna*. We went (wearing boy's clothes) out, joined the other *Fianna*, and walked about the streets whistling rebel tunes. Whenever we passed a British soldier we made him take to the gutter, telling him the streets of Dublin were no place 'for the likes of him.'

The boys took me for one of themselves, and some

began to tell me their deeds of prowess in Dublin. Ever since the war began they had gone about to recruiting meetings, putting speakers to rout and sometimes upsetting the platforms.[2] This sounds like rowdyism, but it is only by such tests of courage and strength that the youth of a dominated race can acquire the self-confidence needed later for the real struggle.

They sang for me Madam's 'Anti recruiting Song', which they always used as an accompaniment to their attacks on recruiting booths. Its first two lines go thus:

> The recruiters are raidin' old Dublin, boys!
> It's them we'll have to be troublin', boys!

And the last two lines are:

> From a Gael with a gun the Briton will run!
> And we'll dance at the wake of the Empire, boys!

These disturbances by the *Fianna* were part of a campaign by which Nationalists hoped to keep Irishmen out of the war and ready for their own fight when the time came. Many were kept at home, but hundreds were thrown out of work by their employers with the direct purpose of making them enter the British army,

---

2. The First World War began in August 1914. Recruitment efforts in Ireland were fierce. The Irish Citizen Army, *Fianna Eireann* and remaining Irish Volunteers were all against the war and employed anti-recruitment tactics. A majority of the Irish Volunteers signed up for the British Army in August 1914, believing their actions would ensure Home Rule for Ireland. It caused a split in the organisation and the Irish Volunteers that remained behind kept the name and participated in Easter Week.

had to enlist for the pitiful 'King's Shilling'. Nothing so illustrates the complete lack of humour of the British as their method of arousing interest in the war. They declared it was the part of England to 'defend the honour and integrity of small nations'!

Even before the war the countess had watched for any opportunity to destroy militarist propaganda. Although England has won the world's heart by explaining she never considered there was danger of war, and for that reason the preparedness of her enemy was an unfair advantage, still, we had heard of the German menace for a long time. It was announced in Dublin that the play, *An Englishman's Home*, which had had a long run in London, where it pictured to thousands the invasion of England by the Germans, was to open for an equally long run in the Irish capital to stir us to take precautions against invasion.

Madam took her *Fianna* boys in full force to the opening night performance.[3] They occupied pit and gallery while the rest of the theatre was filled with British officers and their wives. The fine uniforms and evening dress made a great showing, for Dublin is the most heavily garrisoned city of its size in the world.

The play went on peacefully enough until the Germans appeared on the stage. At their first appearance as the invading foe, the *Fianna*, in green shirts and saffron kilts, stood up and sung in German, 'The Watch on the Rhine', just as the countess had taught it to them.

Of course there was consternation, but after a moment an officer stood up and began to sing 'God Save

---

3. This opening night performance was on 3 May 1909 in the Theatre Royal, Hawkins Street, Dublin.

the King'. All the other officers and the 'ascendancy people', as we call our English upper class in Ireland, rose and joined him. But you cannot safely sing 'God Save the King' in Dublin. Eggs and vegetables at once began to fly, and the curtain had to be rung down. So ended the Dublin run of *An Englishman's Home*![4]

These things the *Fianna* boys told me on our way to the shooting gallery where they wanted to see the Glasgow 'boy' shoot. I hit the bullseye oftener than any of them, much to the delight of the boy who knew I was a girl. He was not much surprised, however, for by her own skill Madam had accustomed them to expect good marksmanship in a woman.

---

4. Irish Nationalist disruption of plays was a common feature of the early 20th century in Dublin. In 1907, there was a riot in response to JM Synge's *The Last Playboy of the Western World*. In 1926, there were similar disruptions of Sean O'Casey's drama *The Plough and the Stars*. The latter was led by some of the mothers and widows of the men executed in Easter week who felt that the depiction of the Easter week rebels in the play was shameful.

2

AS THIS WAS my first visit to Dublin, Madam thought I might want to see some of the sights. She took me to a museum and next suggested that we visit an art gallery.

'What I really want to see,' I told her, 'is the poorest part of Dublin, the very poorest part.'

This pleased her for her heart is always there. She took me to Ash Street.[5] I do not believe there is a worse street in the world than Ash Street. It lies in a hollow where sewage runs and refuse falls; it is not paved and is full of holes. One might think it had been under shellfire. Some of the houses have fallen down – from sheer weariness it seems, while others are shored up at the sides with beams. The fallen houses look like corpses, the others like cripples leaning upon crutches.

Dublin is full of such streets, lanes, and courts where houses, years ago condemned by the authorities, are still tenanted. These houses are symbolic of the downfall of Ireland. They were built by rich Irishmen for their homes. Today they are tenements for the poorest Irish people, but they have not been remodelled for this purpose, and that is one reason why they seem

---

5. Ash Street is in the area known as The Liberties in central Dublin. It is only a five minute walk from St Patrick's Cathedral.

so appalling – the poor among the ruins of grandeur.

In one room, perhaps a drawing room, you find four families, each in its own corner, with sometimes not as much as the tattered curtains for partitions. Above them may be a ceiling of wonderfully modelled and painted figures, a form of decoration the art of which has been lost. At the end of this room is a mantel of purest white marble over an enormous fireplace long ago blocked up, except for a small opening in which a few coals at a time may be burned. The doors of such a room are often made of solid mahogany 15 feet in height.

The gas company of Dublin refuses to furnish gas above the second floor, and the little fireplaces can never give enough heat even when fuel is comparatively plentiful. As I write, coal is $15 a ton, and is costing the poor who buy in small quantities from 30 to 45 per cent more.

In Dublin there are more than 20,000 such rooms in which one or more families are living. That epidemics are not more deadly speaks well for the fundamental health of those who live in them, for there are no sanitary arrangements. Water is drawn from a single tap somewhere in the backyard. The only toilet, to be used by all the people in any one of these houses, is also in the backyard or worse still, in a dark unventilated basement.

The head of a family in these one-time 'mansions,' which number several thousand seldom makes more than four or five dollars a week! Of this amount, if they want the luxury of even a small room to themselves, they must pay about a dollar. Is it any wonder that the word 'rent' has a fearful sound to the Irish? After this rent is paid there is not much left for food and clothes. Starvation, even in time of peace, is always hovering near. Bread and tea for breakfast, but rarely butter; bread and tea and either herrings or potatoes, sometimes with cabbage, for their mid-day meal; bread and tea for supper. Two fifths of the inhabitants of Dublin live on this fare the year round. If they have beef or mutton once a week they must eat it boiled or fried, since the fireplaces are too primitive for roasting or baking. Neither will they permit baking of bread or cakes.

Yet Ireland could raise fruit and vegetables and grain for 20 million people! I have seen ships deep laden with food for need of which the Irish are slowly starving – I contend undernourishment is starvation – going in a steady stream to England. The reason was that the English were able to pay better prices than the man at home. Food, since the beginning of the war, has literally been drained out of the country. Ireland today is in a state of famishment, if not of famine.

Here in Dublin though the streets and lanes seem full of children, the death rate is tremendously high. The population of all Ireland has decreased 50 per cent in 50 years. In Poland, under the rule of the Russian czar the population increased. It is one thing to read about Irish 'grievances', it is another to be living where they go on year after year.

'Grievance' – that is the way the British sum up our sense of wrong and with such effect that people the world over fancy our wrongs are not wrongs but imagined grievances. The word itself counts against us in the eyes of those who have never been to Ireland and seen for themselves the conditions under which the great majority of the population must live. To be sure, there are always complaints carried to Parliament and then a 'commission of inquiry', followed a little later by a 'report upon conditions'. But the actual results seem small. It was disgust for this sort of carrying out complaints in a basket and bringing back reports in the very same basket that roused Arthur Griffith to write his pamphlet on Hungary and her rebuilding from within. He felt that the Irish, too, must set about saving themselves without political help from parliamentarians. He even went so far as to say that, since Irishmen who went to Parliament seemed so soon to forget their country except as it served their political advancement, we ought not to send men to Parliament.[6] Ireland, he declared, should concentrate upon the economic and industrial life possible to her – a life that could be developed wonderfully if men set out to win Ireland for the Irish. This propaganda of Griffith's – for it soon became such – stirred all the young men and women who before had been hopeless. 'Ireland for the Irish!'. The movement quickly became what is called the '*Sinn Féin*', which is Gaelic for 'Ourselves Alone'.[7]

That this organisation should be considered in America as a sort of 'Black Hand', or anarchistic society, is evidence of the impression it made upon the

---

6. This would be put into practice in January 1919, when *Sinn Féin* won 73 of the 105 seats in Ireland in the 1918 General Election. The party refused to take their seats in London and instead set up their own Parliament in Dublin, known as the *Dáil Éireann*.

7. This is a frequent mistranslation. Correctly, it is 'We Ourselves'.

English as a powerful factor to be reckoned with. It had come into being overnight, but its principles were as old as Ireland. It sprang from a love of Ireland and not, as many believe, from hatred of England. It could not have thrived as it did wherever it touched a young heart and brain if it had merely been a protest It had a national ideal and goal. Every day was dedicated to it. To speak the Irish language; to wear Irish made clothes of Irish tweed; to think and feel, write, paint, or work for the best interests of Ireland; to make every act, personal or communal, count for the betterment of Ireland – all this was animated by love of our country. The *Sinn Féin* was constantly inspired by poems and essays which appeared in Arthur Griffith's weekly magazine.[8] That poetry today is known throughout civilisation as the poetry of the 'Celtic Revival'.

There was a gospel of 'passive resistance', too, which led Irishmen to refuse to pay taxes or take any part in the anglicising of Ireland. It was this phase that soon won the disapproval of the party that stood for parliamentary activity and naturally it aroused dissatisfaction in England.

From Ash Street the countess took me to Glasnevin Cemetery, where men lie buried, who, having lived under conditions such as I had just looked upon, spent their lives in protest against the same. Here was the grave of O'Donovan Rossa and a score of others whom I felt were heroes. Here, also, was the grave of Anne Devlin, that brave woman who refused to betray Robert Emmet to the British officers seeking him after

---

8. The journal *Sinn Féin* was supressed by the British in 1914 at the outbreak of the First World War.

his unsuccessful effort to oppose English rule in 1803. These graves and the ruinous houses of Ash Street show patriotism and poverty working for each other and, despite themselves, against each other.

A few months after my visit, there was fighting all about Glasnevin Cemetery between the Royal Irish Constabulary and those who were to carry on the traditions of the great struggle.

Not far from the home of Countess Markievicz stand the Portobello barracks, while much farther off are the Beggar's Bush barracks. She asked me one day if I thought I could make a plan of the latter from observation that would be of use if at any time it was decided to dynamite them. She gave no explanation, did not even tell me in what part of Dublin the barracks were located nor that two officers of the Irish Volunteers had already tried to make this plan and had failed. But she knew that I had had experience in gaining distances and drawing maps. I had just taken a course in calculus, and it was when telling her of my love for mathematics that she set me this task.

There was a large map of Dublin on the wall of a study in her house. I scrutinised this carefully, for I did not know my way alone about Dublin. Then I started out and found the place without great difficulty. It is in the southwestern outskirts of the city, a large brick structure filling in the right angle where two streets meet. From this corner I walked very slowly along the front of the barracks, counting my paces, gaining the height of the outer wall, and studying the building itself for anything its secretive exterior might betray. I presently noticed that the loopholes which appeared in the wall at regular intervals stopped short a number of yards from the corner. They had been filled in with bricks of a slightly different colour than the rest of the wall. At once I asked myself why this had been done and, to discover the reason, if possible, crossed the street to where I could look over the wall. I was able to see that within the right angle at the corner was a small, circular building. It stood close to both the front and side wall, yet did not touch either. There was room for a sentry to walk around it, and all loopholes near it had been bricked up.

The conclusion I drew from this fact was that here was a powder magazine. It was so placed as not to be too noticeable from the street, easily guarded by a sentry, and conveniently near the loopholes in case defence of the barracks became necessary.

I walked away and next approached the barracks from another side. Here I found that between the street and the main wall was a low outer wall about my own height. When I reached the spot where I thought the magazine ought to be, I took my handkerchief and let it blow – accidentally, of course – over this outer wall. A passing boy gallantly offered to get it for me. Being a woman and naturally curious, I found it necessary to pull myself up on tiptoe to watch him as he climbed over the wall. The ground between the two walls had not been paved but was of soft earth. I had seen enough. Thanking the boy, I put my handkerchief carefully into my pocket so as not to trouble anyone else by making them climb about on Dublin walls and went on my way.

Upon my return to Leinster Road I gave the distances and heights I had taken to Madam, describing the way a hole could be dug, under cover of a dark night, between the two walls close to where the magazine stood. A quantity of explosive could be placed in this hole, a long wire could be attached to a detonator and laid along the outer wall for some distance, and then without being noticed, someone could touch the end of the wire with the battery from a pocket flash lamp. The explosion that followed, I felt sure, would blow up not only the inner wall, but the wall of the magazine and set off the powder stored therein. Madam asked me to write this all down. Later she showed what I had written to the man who was to be Commander-in-chief of the Republican army in Dublin, James Connolly. He knew Beggar's Bush barracks well enough[9] to see that my map was correct and believed the plan practicable enough to carry out in case conscription should become a fact in Ireland despite all promises to the contrary.

But the test I had been put to was, it seemed, not merely a test of my ability to draw maps and figure distances. From that day I was taken into the confidence of the leaders of the movement for making Ireland a republic.

The situation, I learned from Mr Connolly, was very hopeful, because for the first time in hundreds of years those who were planning a revolution to free Ireland had organised bodies of Irish men who not only were well trained in the use of firearms, but so full of the spirit of the undertaking that they were ready at a

---

9. James Connolly had been stationed in Beggar's Bush barracks in June 1886 whilst a soldier in the British Army.

moment's notice to mobilise. There was the Irish Citizen Army which Mr Connolly had organised after the Transport Workers' strike to defend workingmen from onslaughts by the police. I do not believe anyone who has not seen what we call a 'baton charge' of the Dublin police can quite comprehend the motives which make for such ruthless methods.

In the first place, whenever the police are called out for strike duty or to be on the lookout for rioting, they are given permission to drink all they wish. At the station houses are big barrels of porter from which the police are expected to help themselves freely. Then the saloonkeepers – we call them 'publicans' – are not expected to refuse a drink to any policeman who demands it, and are paid or not according to the mood of the protector of the public peace. Add to this that the police do not attack in order to disperse a crowd, but to kill. In a public square where a crowd has gathered to hear a labour speech, the police assemble on four sides and, upon a given signal, rush to the centre, pushing even innocent passers-by into the midst of the crowd that, on the instant, has become a mob. Then the police use their batons like shillelaghs,[10] swinging them around and around before bringing them down upon the heads of the people.

Fearing one of these baton attacks, Madam, having come down to the square in her car, had just stepped out upon the sidewalk when she was struck full in the face by a policeman's club! On that same day, too, the police rushed into the adjoining streets and clubbed

---

10. A wooden walking stick and club with a round knob at the top. Traditionally made from blackthorn.

every person they met, even people several blocks from the square who, at the moment, were coming out of church from vesper service.

Mr Connolly found that in any strike in Ireland the interests of England and of the employer were the same; that his strikers had to meet the two members of the opposition without any defence. Therefore he had organised the men who were fighting for better hours and wages into a 'Citizen Army'. It is against the law for anyone to bear arms in Ireland, but in this case the authorities could do nothing because they had not disarmed the men of Ulster when the latter armed and drilled to defend themselves against Home Rule, should it become a fact. The Ulstermen were openly planning insurrection under Sir Edward Carson – insurrection against a law, a political measure desired by the majority. It was an anarchistic outbreak that Carson had in mind. Mr Connolly, on the other hand, was organising simply for defence against police power that had grown unbridled in its activities.

No one interfered with him. As always, this organisation was under surveillance, and reports about it were sent to the authorities. But there appeared to be no more than 300 members, a small body not dangerous to the police if it should come into conflict with them. It was not known that there were several times 300 members, but that only this number was allowed to drill or march at any one time. This drilling baffled the police. Many a night the 300 would be mobilised and quietly march through Dublin out into the country, the police trailing wearily and nervously after them, expecting some excitement along the line of march. Nothing ever happened. Back to town in the wee small hours the police would come, only to see the men disperse as quietly as they had assembled and go home to bed. After this had happened many times it no longer attracted official attention. Only perfunctory reports were made of any mobilisation of the Citizen Army, and thus it came about that on Easter Sunday the mobilisation was taken for nothing more than the usual drill and not reported.

The second organisation, the Irish Volunteers, was brought into being by those in favour of Home Rule, and was a makeweight against the Ulstermen. Since the Irish Volunteers were organised to protect law, to uphold Home Rule should it become a fact as promised, nothing could be done by the authorities when the volunteers began to arm themselves. Besides, nothing had been done to prevent the Ulstermen from arming themselves. The conservative press in England actually supported the Ulstermen, and English army officers resigned rather than disarm them. What, then, could they be expected to do to a body of men who stood for law and order instead of opposing it as in Ulster? This situation made possible a strategic position for the leaders of the Republican movement.

Had not the authorities realised that now they would meet with armed resistance if they broke their promise about conscription, we should have had to send our brothers to France and Flanders early in the war. But the Citizen Army and the Irish Volunteers had no intention of allowing men to be carried off to fight England's battles when, for the first time in many years, there was a chance of winning freedom for Ireland. To keep this constantly in the public mind, Mr Connolly had a large sign hung over the main entrance to Liberty Hall, his headquarters:

> WE SERVE NEITHER KING NOR KAISER,
> BUT IRELAND

3

THE NEED OF explosives was great, and I took part in a number of expeditions to obtain them. One night we raided a ship lying in the river. The sailors were drunk and three or four of our men had no trouble in getting into the hold. I was standing guard on the other side of the embankment wall, holding one end of a string that served as a telegraph between our outposts in the street and our men in the boat. One jerk from me meant, 'Someone coming'; two jerks, 'Police'; three jerks, 'Clear out as best you can'.

Suddenly I heard the outpost up the street whistling a patriotic tune. This was a signal to me. It meant the police were coming. I gave two jerks of the string and waited.

A policeman came slowly toward me. He had his dark lantern and catching sight of me, flashed it in my face. He stared, but said nothing. No doubt he was wondering what a decently dressed girl was doing in that part of town at such an hour. I watched him as closely as he watched me. If he caught sight of my string, I intended to give three jerks, and, at the same moment, throw pepper in his face, my only weapon.

But he did not notice the string and passed on. My heart had stopped beating; now it began again, though

I felt rather queer. Risks like this have to be taken, however, when one is preparing a revolution and has neither fire arms nor ammunition, the people in power having put an embargo upon them. It is all in the way of war. I can add that this raid was as successful as usual.

One day the countess took several of us including her dog Poppet, out beyond Dundrum. Upon our return we could call this expedition 'a little shooting party'. And it would be the truth, for Poppet, being an Irish cocker, more interested in hunting than in revolts, joined himself to two men who were intent on getting birds. He was of so great assistance that these men, in recognition of his services, gave us a few of the birds he brought in. We took them home as trophies.

But the whole truth was that we had been out to test dynamite. We were looking for some old wall to blow up, and found one on the side of a hill. After the hunters had disappeared, two of us were posted with field glasses while Madam set off the explosive. It was a lonely place, so we were not disturbed. The great stones flew into the air with dust and thunder. Indeed the country people round about, when they heard that rumble and saw the cloud of smoke, must have wondered at the sudden thunderstorm on the hill.

An Irishman told me once that although he had hoped for a revolution and worked for it, he had never felt it would be a reality until one night when he and some friends, out cross-country walking in the moonlight, came upon Madam and her *Fianna* boys bivouacked in the open. They had come out for a drill. She was in uniform, with knee breeches, puttees and officer's coat, and the whole scene was martial and intense.

The *Fianna* were proud of the fact that they were the first military organisation in Ireland, four years older than either the Irish Citizen Army or the Irish Volunteers. It was in 1909 that the countess heard of Baden-Powell coming to Ireland to organise his British Boy Scouts, where they might be useful later on to the empire. She tried to get people interested in organising the same way for Ireland, and finally made this her own task, though she knew nothing of military tactics and as little of boys. There was virtually no money or equipment like that in Baden-Powell's organisation, and naturally many blunders were made at the outset. But she studied both boys and tactics, and finally came to believe that to succeed, the spirit of old Ireland must be invoked.

So the organisation was given the historic Gaelic name, *Fianna*, with its flavour of romance and patriotic tradition. The boys saved up their money for uniforms and equipment, and from the beginning were aware of themselves as an independent, self-respecting body. They have stood well the test of the revolution.

One of the most popular actresses at the Abbey Theatre in Dublin was Helena Molony. Through her energy Mr Connolly returned from America to organise the workingmen of Ireland, and thus met the countess. From the friendship and cooperation of these three persons you can judge how all class distinction had gone down before the love of Ireland and the determination to free her.

James Connolly was a very quiet man at the time I

met him, quiet and tense. He was short and thickset, with a shrewd eye and determined speech. He proved a genius at organisation, and this was lucky, for in Dublin there are no great factories, except Guinness, to employ large numbers of men, and this makes organisation difficult. To have managed such a strike as the Transport Workers' in 1913, after only half a dozen years of organisation is proof of his great ability. And then to organise a Citizen's Army!

Connolly is the answer to those who think the Rising was the work of dreamers and idealists. No one who knew him could doubt that when he led his army of workingmen into battle for the Irish Republic, he believed there was a good fighting chance to establish such a republic. He was practical, and had no wish to spill blood for the mere glory of it; there was nothing melodramatic about him. A north of Ireland man – he originally came from the only part of Ireland I know well, County Monaghan – he had many times given proof of sound judgment and courage. He was often at the house of the countess while I was visiting her and one evening, just before I left, Madam called my attention to the fact that he was in better spirits than for a long time past. Word had come to him from America that on or near Easter Sunday a shipful of arms and ammunition would arrive in Ireland. This news determined the date of the Rising, for it was all that was needed from without to insure success. We believed this then, and do still.

We were collecting and hiding what arms and ammunition we could. In proportion to the amount of courage of those in the secret, so the dynamite that they hid against the day soon to come grew and accumulated. Though the house in Leinster Road was always watched, the countess had it stocked like an arsenal. Bombs and rifles were hidden in absurd places, for she had the skill to do it and escape detection. A French journalist who visited Dublin shortly before the insurrection possibly came upon some of this evidence, or perhaps it was only the *Fianna* uniforms which impressed him, for he wrote, 'The salon of the Countess Markiewicz is not a salon. It is a military headquarters.'

Despite this martial ardour, Madam found time to write poetry and 'seditious' songs. This poetry would be in print now had not the house of Mrs Wise-Power, where she left it for safe keeping, been blown to pieces by English gunners when they tried to find the range of the Post Office. Their marksmanship would not have been so poor, perhaps, had they had the countess to teach them.

Many of the singers of our old and new lays are in prison, sentenced for their part in stirring up insurrection, even though they had nothing to do with the Rising itself. The authorities seemed to take no notice of these patriotic concerts while they were being given, but afterward they paid this modern minstrelsy the tribute it deserved. For these concerts were full of inspiration to everyone who attended. Though all were in the open, they were, as a matter of fact, 'seditious,' if that word means stirring up rebellion against those who rule you against your will.

One of the many things I recall gives a clear idea of the untiring and never-ending enthusiasm of the countess. She realised one day that the Christmas cards usually sold in Ireland were 'made in Germany', and since the war was on, had been supplanted by cards 'made in England'. She sat down at once to design Irish Christmas cards for the holiday season of 1916. But when that Christmas came around she was in prison, and the cards were – no one can say where.

When I left Dublin to return to my teaching in Glasgow, they made me promise that I would come back whenever they sent for me, probably just before Easter.

4

WHEN I TOLD my mother on my return of the plans for Easter, she shook her head.

'There never was an Irish Rising that someone didn't betray it,' she said. 'It was so in '67, and before that in 1798.'

But she did not appreciate the spirit I had found in Dublin. I told her that all were united, rich and poor, dock workers, schoolteachers, poets and bartenders. They were working together; I believed they would stand and fight together. And I was right.

It was not easy to go quietly back to teaching mathematics and hear only now and then what was going on in Dublin. Fortunately, Glasgow is two fifths Irish. Indeed, there are as many Irish there as in Dublin itself, and the spirit among the younger generation is perhaps more intense because we are a little to one side and thus afraid of becoming outsiders.

In February, when conscription came to Scotland, there was nothing for members of the Irish Volunteers in Glasgow to do but to disappear. I knew one lad of 17 whose parents, though Irish, wanted him to volunteer in the service of the empire. He refused, telling them his life belonged to Ireland. He went over to fight at the time of the Rising, and served a year in prison afterwards.

Whenever an Irish Volunteer was notified to report for service in the Glasgow contingent of the British army, he would slip across the same night to Ireland, and go to Kimmage, where a camp was maintained for these boys. While the British military authorities were hunting for them in Scotland and calling them 'slackers,' they were drilling and practising at the target, or making ammunition for a cause they believed in and for which they were ready to die.

Presently news came from Dublin that James Connolly had written a play entitled, *Under Which Flag?*. We heard also that when it was produced, it had a great effect upon the public. In this play the hero, during the last act, chooses the flag of the republic and the final curtain falls. Someone told Mr Connolly he ought to write another act to show what happened afterward. His reply was that another act would have to be written by 'all of us together.'

I know that many people in this country have seen the Irish Players and felt their work was a great contribution to the drama, but I doubt if anyone here can realise what it means to see upon the stage a play dealing with your hopes and fears just at a time when one or the other are about to be realised. For ten years the world has watched with interest as these plays were staged, as poetry appeared which seemed to have a new note in it. The world called it a 'Celtic Revival'. England, too, was interested, for these Irish playwrights, poets and painters served to stimulate her own artists. What if some of the sagas, revived by archaeologists, did picture Irish heroism? What if the theme of play or poem was a free Ireland? What if schoolboys under a

Gaelic name did play at soldiering?

'Dangerous?' someone asked.

'Nonsense!' retorted mighty England. 'Would poets, pedagogues and dreamers dare to lead the Irish people against the imperial power that had dominated them for centuries? Unthinkable!'

England has never understood us so little as in these last ten years. Our pride was growing tremendously – pride not in what we have, but in what we are. The Celtic Revival was only an expression of this new pride.

It was on 18 April that a member of the Dublin town council discovered that the British meant to seize all arms and ammunition of the Irish Volunteers and Irish Citizen Army. History was repeating itself. It was on an 18th of April that American colonists discovered the British intention of seizing their arms and ammunition at Concord. In both cases revolt was made inevitable by this action.

What the reason was that led immediately to such an order being given to the British military authorities in Dublin, I do not know. It had to do with conscription, of course, and it may have been quickened by the resistance of the Irish Citizen Army to the police. Madam told me that, a short time before, the police had attempted one noon to raid Liberty Hall while they supposed the place was empty. By the merest accident, she and Mr Connolly, with one or two others, were still there. The object of the raid was to get possession of the press on which was printed *The Workers' Republic*, a paper published at the hall by Mr Connolly.

When the first members of the police force entered,

Connolly asked them if they had a warrant. They had none. He told them they could not come in without one. At the same time the countess quietly drew her revolver and as quietly pointed it in their direction in a playful manner. They understood her, however, and quickly withdrew to get their warrant.

Immediately Connolly sent an order for the Citizen Army to mobilise. How they came! On the run, slipping into uniform coats as they ran; several from the tops of buildings where they were at work, others from underground. More than one, thinking this an occasion of some seriousness, instantly threw up their jobs.

By the time the police returned with their warrant, the Irish Citizen Army was drawn up around Liberty Hall, ready to defend it. It was not raided.

Mr Connolly showed me a copy of the secret order when I arrived on Holy Thursday. It read:

> The following precautionary measures have been sanctioned by the Irish Office on recommendation of the General Officer commanding the forces in Ireland. All preparations will be made to put these measures in force immediately on receipt of an order issued from the Chief Secretary's Office, Dublin Castle, and signed by the Under Secretary and the General Officer commanding the forces in Ireland.
>
> First, the following persons will be put under arrest: All members of the *Sinn Féin* National Council, the Central Executive Irish *Sinn Féin* Volunteer County Board, Irish *Sinn Féin* Volunteers, Executive Committee National Volunteers, Coisda Gnótha Com-

mittee[11], Gaelic League. See list A3 and 4 and supplementary list A2.

I interrupt the order to emphasise the fact that we were all listed, and that the '*Sinn Féin*' organisation seemed to attract most attention from the authorities. Indeed, after it was all over, the Rising was often called the *Sinn Féin* Revolt. The *Sinn Féin* was an organisation which had become a menace to Great Britain because of its tactics of passive resistance. The words *Sinn Féin*, as already stated, mean 'ourselves alone', and the whole movement was for an Irish Ireland.

The *Sinn Féin*ers are likened to the 'Black Hand' or other anarchistic groups by those who read of them as leaders of a 'revolt'. As a matter of fact, they were, from the first, the literary, artistic and economic personalities who started the Celtic Revival. Arthur Griffiths, who is not given enough credit for the passion with which he conceived the idea of working for Ireland as Hungarians worked for Hungary, published a little weekly magazine in which the first of the new poetry appeared. It appealed to the deepest instincts in us; it was a revolt of the spirit, clothing itself in practical deed.

But it was not a negative program. The refusal to do or say or think in the anglicised way, as was expected of us, held in it loyalty to something fine and free, the existence of which we believed in because we had read of it in the history of Ireland in our sagas. We were not

---

11. The executive committee of the Gaelic League. Most of the signatories of the Proclamation of the Irish Republic were members of the Gaelic League (*Conradh na Gaeilge*). Eoin Mac Néill was President of the Gaelic League in 1916.

a people struggling up into an untried experience, but a people regaining our kingdom, which at one time in the history of mankind had been called 'great' wherever it was known of or rumoured.

This was the feeling that animated the groups listed by British military men as the '*Sinn Féin* National Council' and 'Central Executive and *Coisda Gnótha* Committee of the Gaelic League,' but which to an outsider cannot, without explanation, give any idea of the fire and fervour implanted in committee and council.

But to return to the document. It went on:

> An order will be issued to the inhabitants of the city to remain in their homes until such time as the Competent Military Authority may otherwise direct and permit.
>
> Pickets chosen from units of Territorial Forces will be at all points marked on maps 3 and 4. Accompanying mounted patrols will continuously visit all points and report every hour.
>
> The following premises will be occupied by adequate forces and all necessary measures used without need of reference to Headquarters:
>
> First, premises known as Liberty Hall, Beresford Place; No. 6 Harcourt Street, *Sinn Féin* Building; No. 2 Dawson Street, Headquarters Volunteers; No. 12 D'Olier Street, Nationality Office; No. 25 Rutland Square, Gaelic League Office; No. 41 Rutland Square, Foresters' Hall; *Sinn Féin* Volunteer premises

in city; All National Volunteer premises in city; Trades Council premises, Capel Street; Surrey House, Leinster Road, Rathmines.

The following premises will be isolated, all communication to or from them prevented: Premises known as the Archbishop's House, Drumcondra; Mansion House, Dawson Street; No. 40 Herbert Park, Ballyboden; Saint Enda's College, Hermitage, Rathfarnham; and, in addition, premises in list 5D, see maps 3 and 4.

This order should become a classic, because it is such a good list of all meeting places of those who loved and worked for Ireland in the last few years. Even the home of the countess, Surrey House, was to have been occupied; and Saint Enda's, the school where Pádraig Pearse was headmaster and chief inspiration, was to be 'isolated'.

Had there been any question about a rising, the possession of this secret order to the military authorities in Dublin would have been the signal for it. It was not to be expected that these headquarters of all that was Irish in the city would surrender tamely to 'occupation'. More than this, the order gave new determination to a secret organisation not mentioned in it, the Irish Republican Brotherhood. Not that this was a new organisation, or unknown to the British, for, in its several phases, it had been in existence since 1858. Its oath is secret, yet has been published in connection with disclosures about the *Fenian* movement. This was one of the names it bore, before the Rising of 1867 betrayed it to the Government. So at this time Connolly and Pádraig Pearse and MacDonagh, with all those working to free Ireland, were members of this brotherhood and the republic seemed nearer becoming a reality than ever before in the history of the long struggle.

At Liberty Hall I saw the flag of the republic waiting to be raised. I saw, too, the bombs and ammunition stored there and was set to work with some other girls making cartridges. This was on the Thursday before Easter. That same evening I was given a dispatch to take to Belfast. The address of the man to whom it was to be delivered was at Mr Connolly's home in the outskirts of the city. I was to go there first and get it from Nora Connolly, then go on to this man.

I had never been in Belfast and when I reached the city, it was two o'clock in the morning. The streets were dark and deserted. I finally had to ask a policeman which of the few cars running would take me to that part of town where the Connollys lived. I wonder what he would have done had he guessed I was bent upon revolutionary business. There is something very weird in knowing that while things are going on as usual in the outer world, great changes are coming unawares.

I rang in vain when I reached the house. Could all the family be somewhere else? Could I have made a mistake? I was beginning to think so when a window opened, and I heard a voice say, 'It's all right, Mother. It's only a girl.' Presently the door opened. They had been afraid that it was the police, for in these last few days before the time set, suspense was keen. At any moment all plans might be given away to the police and everyone arrested. A ring in the middle of the night was terrifying. They had not been to bed; they were making Red Cross bandages and learning details of equipment and uniform for the first aid girls. They had slept little for days, now that the time of the Rising approached.

We did not dare go out again in the dead of night to hunt up the man for whom I had brought my dispatch. This action would create suspicion. So about five o'clock, just when the working people were beginning to go about their tasks, we took the street car, went into another part of Belfast, and found him.

Mrs Connolly and the girls went back to Dublin with me. They were to be there during the revolt, and did not know if they would ever see their home again; but they dared not take anything with them except the clothes on their backs. Always no suspicion must be aroused; it must look as if they were starting off for the Easter holidays.

This was not an easy leave-taking, for there was a fair chance of the house being sacked and burned. Mrs Connolly went about, picking up little things that would go in her trunk but the absence of which would not be noticed if any inquisitive policeman came in to see whether anything suspicious was going on. As we left, none of them looked back or gave any show of feeling. Revolution makes brave actors.

That afternoon I was again at ammunition work. This time my duty was to go about Dublin, taking from hiding places dynamite and bombs secreted therein. Once, on my way back to Liberty Hall with some dynamite wrapped in a neat bundle on the seat beside me, I heard a queer, buzzing noise. It seemed to come from inside the bundle.

'Is it going off?' I asked myself, and sat tight, expecting every moment to be blown to bits. But nothing happened; it was only the car wheels complaining as we passed over an uneven bit of track.

5

IT WAS ON Saturday morning that I heard the news of our first defeat – a defeat before we had begun. The ship with arms and ammunition that had been promised us while I was in Dublin at Christmas, had come into Tralee Harbour and waited 21 hours for the Irish Volunteers of Tralee to come and unload her. But it had attracted no attention except from a British patrol boat, and so had to turn about and put to sea again. There upon, the suspicions of the officials having led them to set out after the *Aud*, she had shown her German colours and, in full sight of the harbour, blew herself up rather than allow her valuable cargo to fall into the hands of the British.[12]

Besides several machine guns, 20,000 rifles and a million rounds of ammunition were aboard that ship. For every one of those rifles we could have won a man to carry it in the rebellion. Thus their loss was an actual loss of fighting strength.

It all was a blunder that now seems like fate. The

---

12. The *Aud* was in actual fact the SS *Castro*, which was acquired from the British Navy in 1914 by the Imperial German Navy and renamed the SMS *Libau*. A merchant steam ship, it masqueraded as the similar Norwegian ship, the SS *Aud*, for the purpose of delivering arms to Ireland.

Aud, as first planned, was to arrive on Good Friday. Then the leaders decided it would be better not to have her arrive until after the Rising had begun, or on Easter. Word of this decision was sent to America, to be forwarded to Germany. This was done, but the *Aud* had just sailed, keeping to her original schedule. She carried no wireless, and so could not be reached at sea.

I often think the heroic determination of that captain to sink his ship and crew must have been preceded by many hours of bitterest chagrin and anxiety. He could not have had the slightest idea why the plan was not being carried out. It would have been, too, had the Volunteers at Tralee, remembering the uncertainty of all communication, been on watch for fear the countermanding order might have miscarried.[13]

But it was too late now to draw back, even had the leaders so desired. I do not believe that idea ever entered their heads, for their course of action had been long planned. Two men, however, were uncertain of the wisdom of going on with it. One of them, The O'Rahilly,[14] was minister of munitions in the provisional government and felt the loss keenly, because his entire plan of work had been based on this cargo now at the bottom of the ocean. When he found that the majority

---

13. The Captain, Karl Spindler, was interred for the duration of the war. Spindler later wrote a book about this incident entitled *Gun Running For Roger Casement: In the Easter Rebellion of 1916* (London: WH Collins and Sons Ltd, 1921).

14. Michael Joseph O'Rahilly. As Director of Arms for the Irish Volunteers, he personally oversaw the landing of 900 rifles at Howth in July 1914. This was the first major arming of the Volunteers and was a response to the Larne gunrunning by the Ulster Volunteers in 1913.

believed success was still possible, and that the seizure of arms in the British arsenals in Ireland would compensate for the loss, he gave in and worked as whole heartedly as the others. The second man to demur was Professor Eoin MacNeill, who was at the head of the Irish Volunteers as their commander-in-chief. He did not wish to risk the lives of his men against such heavy odds. Yet, when he left the conference, he had not given one hint of actually opposing plans then under discussion.

As I came out of church on Easter morning, I saw placards everywhere to this effect:

NO VOLUNTEER MANOEUVRES TODAY

This was astounding! The manoeuvres were to be the beginning of the revolution. Today they were not to be the usual, simple drill, but the real beginning of military action. All over Ireland the Volunteers were expected to mobilise and stay mobilised until the blow had been struck – until, perhaps, victory had been won. And the Irish Volunteers made up two thirds of our fighting force. 'No Volunteer manoeuvres today'? What could it mean?

I bought a newspaper and read the order of demobilisation, signed by Professor MacNeill. What could have happened? I hurried to Liberty Hall to find the leaders there as much in the dark as I.

They knew MacNeill had been depressed and fearful of results, but they had not supposed him capable of actually calling off his men from the movement so late in the day, though this was quite within his technical rights if he wished. They had taken for granted that he, like The O'Rahilly, would prefer to cast in his lot with the rest of us. I recalled that at Christmas the countess had been eager to have another head chosen for the Volunteers. Over and over again she had said that, though MacNeill had been splendid for purposes of organisation, and the presence of so earnest and pacific a man in command of the Volunteers had prevented England from getting nervous, he was not the man for a crisis. She liked him, but her intuition proved right. He could not bear that his Irish Volunteers should risk their lives and gain nothing thereby. He truly believed they had no chance without the help the *Aud* had promised. As soon as he had published his demobilisation order, he went to his home outside Dublin and stayed there during the Rising. It was there he was arrested and, though his action so helped the British that the royal commission afterward said he 'broke the back of the rebellion' he was sentenced for life, and sits today in Dartmoor Prison making sacks. This is the man who was one of our greatest authorities on early Irish history.

There never was a hint of suspicion that MacNeill's act was other than the result of fear. No one who knew him could doubt his loyalty to Ireland. It was his love for the Volunteers, the love of a man instinctively pacifist, that made him give that order. Oh, the satire of history! By such an order, many of us believe, he delivered to the executioner the flower of Ireland's heart and brain. We believe that if those manoeuvres had taken place at the time set, the British arsenals in Ireland would easily have been taken and arms provided for our men. Indeed, we would rather have taken arms and ammunition from the British than have accepted them as gifts from other people.

The eternal buoyancy with which Irishmen are credited came to their rescue that Sunday morning. Mr Connolly and others believed that if word was sent into the country districts that the Citizen Army was proceeding with its plans, that the Volunteers of Dublin, consisting of four battalions under Pádraig Pearse and Thomas MacDonagh, were going to mobilise, the response would be immediate. At once word was sent out broadcast. Nora Connolly walked 80 miles during the week through the country about Dublin, carrying orders from headquarters. But she, like other messengers, found that the Volunteers were so accustomed to MacNeill's signature that they were afraid to act without it.

They feared a British trick. We Irish are so schooled in suspicion that it sometimes counts against us. In Galway they had heard that the Rising in Dublin was on, and later put up such a fight that, had it been seconded in other counties by even a few groups, the republic would have lived longer than it did. It might even have won the victory in which, only three days before, we all had faith.

The Volunteers numbered men from every class and station; the Citizen Army was made up of working men who had the advantage of being under a man of decision and quick judgment. At four o'clock the Citizen Army mobilised in front of Liberty Hall to carry out the route march as planned. After this march the men were formed into a hollow square in front of

Liberty Hall and Connolly addressed them.

'You are now under arms,' he concluded. 'You will not lay down your arms until you have struck a blow for Ireland!'

The men cheered, shots were fired into the air, and that night their barracks was Liberty Hall.

You might think a demonstration of this character, a speech in the open, would attract enough attention from the police to make them send a report to the authorities. None was sent. They had come to feel, I suppose, that while there was so much talk there would be little action. Nor did they remember that Easter is always the anniversary of that fight hundreds of years ago when native Irish came to drive the foreigner from Dublin. This year, in addition, it fell upon the date of the Battle of Clontarf, so there was double reason for sentiment to seize upon the day for a revolt.[15]

During the night, Irishmen from England and Scotland who had been encamped at Kimmage with some others, came into Dublin and joined the men at Liberty Hall. Next morning I saw them while they were drawn up, waiting for orders. Every man carried a rifle and a pike! Those pikes were admission of our loss through the sinking of the *Aud*, for the men who carried them might have been shouldering additional rifles to give to any recruits picked up during the course of the day. Pikes would not appeal to an unarmed man as a fit weapon with which to meet British soldiers in battle. We could have used every one of those 20,000

15. The Battle of Clontarf occurred on 23 April 1014. It was a decisive victory for the Irish over the Viking power in Ireland, specifically Dublin. The Irish forces were led by Brian Boru, High King of Ireland.

lost rifles, for they would have made a tremendous appeal. I was sent on my bicycle to scout about the city and report if troops from any of the barracks were stirring. They were not. Moreover, I learned that their officers, for the most part, were off to the races at Fairview in the gayest of moods.

When I returned to report to Mr Connolly, I had my first glimpse of Pádraig Pearse, provisional president of the Irish Republic. He was a tall man, over six feet, with broad shoulders slightly stooped from long hours as a student and writer. But he had a soldierly bearing and was very cool and determined, I thought, for a man on whom so much responsibility rested – at the very moment, too, when his dream was about to take form. Thomas MacDonagh was also there. I had not seen him before in uniform, and he, too, gave me the impression that our Irish scholars must be soldiers at bottom, so well did he appear in his green uniform. At Christmas he had given me a fine revolver. It would be one of my proudest possessions if I had it now, but it was confiscated by the British.

I was next detailed as dispatch rider for the St Stephen's Green Command. Again I went out to scout, this time for Commandant Michael Mallin.[16] If I did not find the military moving, I was to remain at the end of the Green until I should see our men coming in to take possession. There were no soldiers in sight; only a policeman standing at the far end of the Green

---

16. Irish socialist and nationalist, Michael Mallin was second in command of the Irish Citizen Army. He had previously served 14 years in the British Army as a drummer in the 21st Royal Scots Fusiliers where he received his military training.

doing nothing. He paid no attention to me; I was only a girl on a bicycle. But I watched him closely. It was impossible to believe that neither the police nor the military authorities were on guard. But this chap stood about idly and was the last policeman I saw until after the Rising was over. They seemed to vanish from the streets of Dublin. Even today no one can tell you where they went.

It was a great moment for me, as I stood there, when, between the budding branches of trees, I caught sight of men in dark green uniforms coming along in twos and threes to take up their position in and about the Green and at the corners of streets leading into it. There were only 36 altogether, whereas the original plan had been for a hundred. That was one of the first effects of Eoin MacNeill's refusal to join us. But behind them I could see, in the spring sunlight, those legions of Irish who made their fight against as heavy or heavier odds and who, though they died, had left us their dream to make real. Perhaps this time...

At last all the men were standing ready, awaiting the signal. In every part of Dublin similar small groups were waiting for the hour to strike. The revolution had begun!

Sackville Street (now O'Connell Street), Dublin, looking towards the General Post Office, c.1900. Skinnider carried dispatches to and from the General Post Office during the Rising.

Parkgate Street, Dublin, in 1910, not far from Kilmainham Jail.

Left: Margaret Skinnider dressed as a boy – she disguised herself to shoot with the *Fianna*. Right: Margaret Skinnider, school teacher.

Countess Markievicz posing for a studio portrait in uniform, c.1915.

Fianna Boys on a field medical training exercise.

Kilmainham Jail, Dublin, in which many of the Volunteers were imprisoned and 14 leaders of the Rebellion executed. (Sean Munson)

The shell of the General Post Office on Sackville Street, Dublin (later O'Connell Street), in the aftermath of the 1916 Rising.

The skeletal remains of the Metropole Hotel, Sackville Street, in May 1916, which was occupied by the Volunteers during the Rising.

Crowds waiting to meet prisoners released under general amnesty. Photograph taken from the railway bridge at Westland Row station (now Pearse Station).
(Wikimedia Commons – appeared on the front page of the *Weekly Irish Times*, Vol. 44, Dublin, Saturday 29 April, 1916)

Linenhall Barracks, Dublin, which had been used by the British Army in the 1870s, was set alight on Edward Daly's orders during the Rising to prevent its reoccupation.

Pádraig Pearse, headmaster, writer and the Irish Republican Brotherhood's spokesperson during the Rising.

Michael Mallin, ICA Commandant. He was much admired by Connolly and one of the few leaders of the rising who readily agreed to allow women to take part.
(National Library of Ireland)
Left: James Connolly.

6

TO THE BRITISH, I am told, there was something uncanny about the suddenness with which the important centres of Dublin's life were quietly seized at noon on Easter Monday by groups of calm, determined men in green uniforms.

They were not merely surprised; they were frightened. The superstitious element in their fear was great, too. It had always been so. When Kitchener was drowned off the Irish coast, a man I know, an Irishman, spoke of it to an English soldier.

'Yes; you and your damned rosaries!' retorted the soldier, looking frightened even as he said it.

The British seem to feel we are in league with unearthly powers against which they have no protection. On Easter Monday they believed that behind this sudden decision, as it appeared to them, something dark and sinister was lurking. How else would we dare to revolt against the British Empire? It was as if our men were not flesh and blood, but spirits summoned up by their own bad conscience to take vengeance for many centuries of misrule. It must have been some such feeling that accounted for the way they lost, at the very outset, all their usual military calm and ruthlessness.

We recognised this feeling, and it made our men

stronger in spirit. We were convinced of the justice of our cause, convinced that even dying was a small matter compared with the privilege we now shared of fighting for that cause. Besides, there was no traitor in our ranks. No one had whispered a word of our plans to the British authorities. That is one reason why our memory of Easter Week has in it something finer than the memory of any other rising in the past. You must bear in mind that the temptation to betray the Rising must have been just as strong, that it had in it just as much guarantee of security for the future, as heretofore. Yet no one yielded to this temptation. Even more amazing was the fact that the authorities had not paid any heed to those utterances which for months past had been highly seditious. For instance, here is what Pádraig Pearse stated openly in one of his articles:

> I am ready. For years I have waited and prayed for this day. We have the most glorious opportunity that has ever presented itself of really asserting ourselves. Such an opportunity will never come again. We have Ireland's liberty in our hands. Or are we content to remain as slaves and idly watch the final extermination of the Gael?

Nothing could be more outspoken or direct. When it is remembered that England's enemies have always been regarded as Ireland's allies; that an English war, wherever fought, is a signal for us to rise once more, no matter how many defeats we have suffered, it might have been supposed the British, stationed in such numbers in and around Dublin, would not have been put to sleep by what must have seemed to the wary observer an acute attack of openness and a vigorous interest in military affairs. There were some, of course, among the police and officials who made their reports of 'highly seditious' meetings and writings, but I suppose the authorities did not believe we would strike.

From America they learned of aid to come by ship when Igel's papers were seized by United States authorities. It may have been this information that put the English patrol boats on their guard in Tralee Harbour. It even may have been thought that when that ship went down the Rising was automatically ended. So it might have been had our revolt been 'made in Germany', but it must be remembered that it was the Irish who approached the Germans. Thus there was no anxiety in Dublin that Easter Monday except as to which horse would win the Fairview races.

As soon as our men were in position in St Stephen's Green I rode off down Leeson Street toward the Grand Canal to learn if the British soldiers were now leaving Beggar's Bush or the Portobello barracks. Everything remained quiet.

That signified to me that our men had taken possession of the Post Office for headquarters and of all other premises decided on in the revised plan of strategy adapted to a much smaller army.

The names of these places do not sound martial. Jacob's Biscuit Factory, Boland's Bakery, Harcourt Street Railway Station and Four Courts are common enough, but each had been chosen for the strategic advantage it would give those defending Dublin with a few men against a great number. The Dublin & South-Eastern

Railway yards, for example, gave control of the approach from Kingstown[17] where, it was expected, the English coming over to Ireland would land.

Again I was sent out to learn if the Harcourt Street Station had been occupied by our men. This had been done and already telegraph wires there, as well as elsewhere, had been cut to isolate Dublin. Telephone wires were cut, too, but one was overlooked. By that wire word of the Rising reached London much sooner than otherwise would have been the case. But here again, the wonder is not that something had been overlooked, but that so much was accomplished. By the original plan, volunteers were told off to do this wire cutting and the hundred and one things necessary to a revolt taking place in a city like Dublin. When this work was redistributed to one third the original number of men, it was hard to be certain that those who had never drilled for the kind of task assigned them could do it at all. This insurrection had been all but rehearsed during those months when it was being worked out on paper by daily and weekly drills.

Upon my return, I found our men entrenching themselves in St Stephen's Green. All carried tools with which to dig themselves in, and shrubbery was used to protect the trenches. Motor cars and drays passing the Green were commandeered, too, to form a barricade. Much to the bewilderment of their occupants, who had no warning that anything was amiss in Dublin, the men in green uniforms would signal them to stop. Except in one instance, they did so quickly enough. Then they were told to get out. An experienced chauffeur among

---

17. Now called Dún Laoghaire.

our men would jump in at once and drive the car to a position where it was needed. The occupants would stand for a moment aghast, then take to their heels. One drayman refused his cart and persisted in his refusal, not believing it when our men told him this was war. He was shot. Two British officers were taken prisoners in one of the autos. We could not afford men to stand guard over them, but we took good care of them. Afterward they paid us the tribute of saying that we obeyed all the rules of war.

Commandant Mallin gave me my first dispatch to carry to headquarters at the General Post Office. As I crossed O'Connell Street, I had to ride through great crowds of people who had gathered to hear Pádraig Pearse read the proclamation of the republic at the foot of Nelson's Pillar. They had to scatter when the Fifth Lancers – the first of the military forces to learn that insurgents had taken possession of the Post Office – rode in among them to attack the Post Office.

Nothing can give one a better idea of how demoralised the British were by the first news of the Rising than to learn that they sent cavalry to attack a fortified building. Men on horseback stood no chance against rifle fire from the windows of the Post Office. It must be said in extenuation, however, that it probably was because this cavalry detachment had just convoyed some ammunition wagons to a place not far from O'Connell Street, and so were sent to 'scatter' men who, they supposed, could be put to flight by the mere appearance of regulars on horseback.

When I reached the open space in front of the Post Office, I saw two or three men and horses lying in the street, killed by the first volley from the building. It was several days before these horses were taken away, and there was something in the sight of the dumb beasts that hurt me every time I had to pass them. It may sound harsh when I say that the thought of British soldiers being killed in the same way did not awaken similar feelings. That is because for many centuries we have been harassed by men in British uniform. They have become to us symbols of a power that seems to delight in tyranny.

Even while I was cycling toward the Post Office, the crowd had reassembled to watch the raising of the flag of the Irish Republic. As the tricolour – green, white and orange – appeared above the roof of the Post Office, a salute was fired. A few days later, while it was still waving, James Connolly wrote, 'For the first time in 700 years the flag of a free Ireland floats triumphantly over Dublin City!'

Mr Connolly and a few of his officers came out to look at it as it waved up there against the sky. I saw an old woman go up to him and, bending her knee, kiss his hand. Indeed, the people loved and trusted him.

Inside the Post Office our men were busy putting things to right after the lancers' attack. They were getting ready for prolonged resistance. Windowpanes were smashed and barricades set up to protect men who soon would be shooting from behind them. Provisions were brought over from Liberty Hall, where they had long been stored against this day. But what impressed me most was the way the men went at it, as though this was the usual sort of thing to be doing and all in the day's work. There was no sign of excitement, but there was a tenseness, a sense of expectancy, a kind of exaltation that was almost more than I could bear.

I delivered my dispatch, and was given another to carry back to Commandant Mallin. Crowds were still in O'Connell Street when I left on my errand. They were always there when bullets were not flying, and always seemed in sympathy with the men in the Post Office. I found this same sympathy all over the city wherever I went. Even when men would not take guns and join us, they were friendly.

The soldiers from Portobello barracks were sent out twice on Monday to attack our position in St Stephen's Green. The first time was at noon, before we were completely entrenched. They had gone only as far as Portobello Bridge, but a few rods from the barracks, when they were fired on from the roof of Davies' public house just the other side of the bridge. Our rifle fire was uninterrupted, and a number of the soldiers fell. They probably thought they were dealing with a considerable force, for they did not advance until the firing ceased or until word was brought to the three men on the roof that we were securely entrenched. Even then they did not come on to attack us, but went somewhere else in the city.

At six o'clock that evening, just when it was beginning to grow dusk, on my way back from the Post Office I noticed that the crowd of curious civilians who had been hanging about the Green all day had quite disappeared. The next thing I saw was two persons hurrying away from the Green. These were Town Councillor Partridge and the countess. They came to a halt in the street just ahead of me. Then I saw the British soldiers coming up Harcourt Street!

The countess stood motionless, waiting for them to come near. She was a lieutenant in the Irish Volunteers[18] and, in her officer's uniform and black hat with great plumes, looked most impressive. At length she raised her gun to her shoulder – it was an 'automatic' over a foot long, which she had converted into a short rifle by taking out the wooden holster and using it as a stock – and took aim. Neither she nor Partridge noticed me as I came up behind them. I was quite close when they fired. The shots rang out at the same moment, and I saw the two officers leading the column drop to the street. As the countess was taking aim again, the soldiers, without firing a shot, turned and ran in great confusion for their barracks. The whole company fled as fast as they could from two people, one of them a woman! When you consider, however, that for years these soldiers had been going about Dublin as if they owned it; that now they did not know from what house or street corner they might be fired upon by men in green uniforms, it is not to be wondered at that they were temporarily demoralised.

As we went back to the Green, Madam told me of the attempt made that morning by herself, Sean Connolly and ten others to enter Dublin Castle and plant the flag of the Irish Republic on the roof of that stronghold of British power in Ireland. There always was a considerable military force housed in the castle, but so completely were they taken by surprise that for a few moments it seemed as if the small group would succeed

---

18. Markievicz was in actual fact a Lieutenant in the Irish Citizen Army, rather than the Volunteers.

in entering. It was only when their leader, Sean Connolly, was shot dead that the attempt was abandoned. It seemed to me particularly fitting that Madam had been a member of this party, for she belonged by 'right of birth' to those who always were invited to social affairs at the castle. Yet she had long refused to accept these invitations, and had taken the side of those who hoped for the ultimate withdrawal of those Dublin Castle hosts.

Immediately after this gallant attempt, which might have succeeded had it taken place on Sunday with the number of men originally intended, Madam returned to St Stephen's Green and alone and singlehanded took possession of the College of Surgeons. This is a big, square, granite building on the west side of the Green. It was, as we later discovered, impregnable. For all the impression they made, the machine gun bullets with which the British soldiers peppered it for five days might have been dried peas.

The countess, fortunately, had met with no resistance. She walked up the steps, rang the bell, and, when no one answered, fired into the lock and entered. The flag we flew from the roof of the building was a small one I had brought on my bicycle from headquarters.

7

WE WERE ALL happy that night as we camped in St Stephen's Green. Despite the handicap we were under through lack of men, almost everything was going our way. It was a cold, damp night. The first aid and dispatch girls of our command went into a summerhouse for shelter. It had no walls, but there was a floor to lie upon, and a roof. I slept at once and slept heavily.

Madam was not so fortunate. She was too tired and excited to sleep. Instead, she walked about, looking for some sheltered place and, to get out of the wind, tried lying down in one of the trenches. But the ground was much too chilly, so she walked about until she noticed the motorcar of her friend, Dr Katherine Lynn, seized that morning for the barricade. She climbed in, found a rug and went to sleep in comparative comfort. When morning came she could not forgive herself for having slept there all night while the rest of us remained outdoors. She had intended to get up after an hour or two of it and make one of us take her place. She did not waken, however, till she heard the hailing of machine gun bullets on the roof of the car. The girls in the summerhouse, with the exception of myself, were awakened at the same moment in the same way, and ran for safety behind one of the embankments. It seems the British had taken possession of a hotel at one side of the Green – the Hotel Shelbourne – and had placed a machine gun on the roof. At four o'clock in the morning they began firing.

The chill had already woken me, but I quickly followed the others to their hiding place. From the first we were aware that had we taken possession of all buildings around the Green, as was our original plan, this morning salute of the British would have been impossible. As it was, our entrenchments and barricades proved of no avail. We realised at once we should have to evacuate the Green and retire into the College of Surgeons.

Commandant Mallin sent me with a dispatch to headquarters. He recognised immediately that a regiment could not hold the Green against a machine gun on a tall building that could rake our position easily.

As soon as I returned, I was sent away again to bring in 16 men guarding the Leeson Street Bridge. If we abandoned the Green before they could join us they would be cut off and in great danger. As I rode along on my bicycle, I had my first taste of the risks of street fighting. Soldiers on top of the Hotel Shelbourne aimed their machine gun directly at me. Bullets struck the wooden rim of my bicycle wheel, puncturing it; others rattled on the metal rim or among the spokes. I knew one might strike me at any moment, so I rode as fast as I could. My speed saved my life, and I was soon out of range around a corner. I was not exactly frightened nor did I feel aware of having shown any special courage. My anxiety for the men I was to bring in filled my mind, for though I was out of range, unless we could find a roundabout way to the College of Surgeons 17 of us would be under fire. To make matters worse, the men were on foot.

After I reached this group and gave the order for their return, I scouted ahead up streets I knew would bring us back safely to the college unless already guarded by the British. It was while I was riding ahead of them that I had fresh evidence of the friendliness of the people. Two men presently approached me. They stepped out into the street and said quietly, 'All is safe ahead.'

I rode back, told the guard, and we moved on more rapidly. At another spot a woman leaned out of her window just as I was passing, 'You are losing your revolver,' she called to me.

She may have saved my life by that warning, for my revolver had torn its way through the pocket of my raincoat, and, in another moment, would have fallen to the ground. Had it been discharged, the result might have been fatal.

As we came to the College of Surgeons and were going in by a side door, the men were just retiring from the Green. Since every moment counted, I had ridden ahead to report to Commandant Mallin, and while he stood listening to me, a bullet whizzed through his hat. He took it off, looked at it without comment and put it on again. Evidently the machine gun was still at work.

One of our boys was killed before we got inside the College of Surgeons. Had the British gunners been better trained for their task we might have lost more, for we were completely at their mercy from the moment they began to fire at dawn until the big door of the college closed, and we took up the defence of our new position in the great stone fortress.

Every time I left the college, I was forced to run the gauntlet of this machine gun. I blessed the enemy's bad marksmanship several times a day. To be sure, they tried hard enough to hit something. Once that day I saw them shooting at our first aid girls, who made excellent targets in their white dresses with large red crosses on them. It was a miracle that none of them was wounded. Bullets passed through one girl's skirt and another girl had the heel of her shoe shot off. If I myself had not seen this happen, I could not have believed that British soldiers would disobey the rules of war concerning the Red Cross.

Mr Connolly had issued orders that no soldier was to be shot who did not have arms, and he did not consider the side arms they always carried as 'arms'. My revolver had been given me for self-defence in case I fell into the hands of any soldiers. I confess that, though I never used it, I often felt tempted when I saw British soldiers going along in twos and threes, bent on shooting any of our men. I was not in uniform, however, and had orders not to shoot except thus clothed and so a member of the Republican Army.

Some of the streets I had to ride through were as quiet and peaceful as if there was no thought of revolution in Dublin, but in others I could hear now and then scattered shots from around some corner. It was more than likely that snipers were trying to hold up a force of British on their way to attack one of our main positions. Sometimes I would hear the rattle of a machine gun, and this warned me that I was approaching a house where the enemy was raking a position held by our men. Generally, however, it was the complete and deathlike emptiness of a street that warned me I was close to a scene of hot fighting. This was not always so, for there were times when the curiosity of the crowd got the better of its caution, and it would push dangerously near the shooting.

Several days elapsed before the people of Dublin became fully aware of the meaning of what was going on. Riots are not rare, and this might well seem to many of them only rioting on a large scale, with some new and interesting features. The poor of Dublin have never been appeased with bread or circuses by the British authorities.[19] They have had to be content with starvation and an occasional street disturbance. But little by little, as I rode along, I could detect a change in attitude. Some became craven and disappeared; in others, it seemed that at last their souls might come out of hiding and face the day.

The spirit at the Post Office was always the same – quiet, cheerful and energetic. I used to stand at the head of the great central staircase waiting for answers to my dispatches and could see the leaders as they went to and fro through the corridor. Pádraig Pearse impressed me by his natural air of command. He was serious, but not troubled, not even when he had to ask for men from the Citizen Army to eke out the scant numbers of his Volunteers for some expedition. No one had thought it would be that way, for the Volunteers

---

19. *Panem et circenses* or bread and circuses, initially referred to superficial, as opposed to political, means of appeasing the populace during the downfall of the Roman Empire.

were originally two to one compared with the Citizen Army. Recruits were coming in every day, but at the most there were not 1,500 men against 20,000 British soldiers stationed in or near Dublin.

Whenever there came a lull in business or fighting, the men would begin to sing either rebel songs or those old lays dear to Irishmen the world over. And sometimes they knelt in prayer, Protestants and Catholics side by side. From the very beginning there was a sense of the religious character in what we were doing. This song and prayer at the Post Office were all natural, devoid of self-consciousness. A gay song would follow a solemn prayer, and somehow was not out of harmony with it.

One source of inspiration at the Post Office was 'old Tom Clarke', who had served 15 years for taking part in the Rising of 1867. His pale, worn face showed the havoc wrought by that long term in an English prison, but his spirit had not been broken.

There was Jo Plunkett, too, pale and weak, having come directly from the hospital where he had just undergone an operation. But he knew what prestige his name would lend to this movement – a name famous for 700 years in Irish history. He looked like death, and he met death a few days later at the hands of the English.

I talked about explosives one day with Sean McDermott and we went together to consult a wounded chemist in a rear room to find out what could be done with chemicals we had found at the College of Surgeons. Sean McDermott was like a creature from another planet who had brought his radiance with him to this one. Everyone felt this and loved him for the courage and sweetness he put into all he did.

The O'Rahilly was another of the striking figures at the Post Office. He was known as one of the handsomest men in Ireland, and, in addition to being head of a famous old clan, had large estates. He had given much property to the cause, and now was risking his life for it. He was killed on the last day of the fighting as he led a sortie into the street at one side of the Post Office.[20] His last words were, 'Goodbye and good luck to you!' He said those words to British prisoners he was setting free because the Post Office had caught fire and the game was up. They afterward told of his kindness and care for them at a moment when he himself was in the greatest possible danger.

I can pass anywhere for a Scotch girl – I have often had to since the Rising – and friends will tell you I am hard-headed and practical, without the least trace of mysticism. Yet, whenever I was in general headquarters in the Post Office I felt, despite commonplace surroundings and the din of fighting, an exalted calm that can be possible only where men are giving themselves unreservedly and with clear conscience to a great cause.

---

20. Moore Street. There is a memorial there to him today inscribed with his last words, written to his wife.

8

SINGING 'SOLDIERS ARE we whose lives are pledged to Ireland', we had withdrawn from St Stephen's Green into the College of Surgeons. Only one of our men had been killed, yet this was a retreat and we knew it. If only we had had enough men to take possession of the Shelbourne Hotel, we need not have yielded the Green. As it was, we wasted no time in mourning, but went to work at once to make ourselves ready for a siege that might last no one knew how long.

Under orders from Commandant Mallin, some of the men began to cut through the walls into adjoining buildings. Others went up on the roof to use their rifles against the British soldiers on top of the Shelbourne. Madam went about everywhere, seeking to find anything that could be of use to us. She discovered 67 rifles, with 15,000 rounds of cartridges; also bandoliers and haversacks. All this had belonged, no doubt, to the training corps of the College of Surgeons, and would have been used against us had we not reached the building first.

On the ground floor of the big building were lecture rooms and a museum; upstairs other classrooms, laboratories and the library. On the third floor were the caretaker's rooms and a kitchen where our first aid and dispatch girls took possession and cooked for the others as long as anything remained to cook. Lastly came the garret up under the roof. To shoot from the roof itself quickly became impossible, since our men were easy targets for the gunners on the Shelbourne. As soon as one of our boys was wounded, we knew they had our range, and decided to cut holes through and directly under the sloping roof. Here we could shoot in perfect safety while remaining unseen.

On Wednesday there was little dispatch bearing to do, so I stood around watching the men up there at work. The countess realised my impatience to be doing my bit, also my hesitation at putting myself forward to ask for permission. Without saying anything to me, she went to Commandant Mallin and told him she thought I could be of use under the roof. He gave his permission at once, and she brought me the answer.

Madam had had a fine uniform of green moleskin made for me. With her usual generosity, she had mine made of better material than her own. It consisted of knee breeches, belted coat and puttees. I slipped into this uniform, climbed up astride the rafters and was assigned a loophole through which to shoot. It was dark there, full of smoke and the din of firing, but it was good to be in action. I could look across the tops of trees and see the British soldiers on the roof of the Shelbourne. I could also hear their shots hailing against the roof and wall of our fortress, for in truth this building was just that. More than once I saw the man I aimed at fall. To those who have been following the Great War, reading of thousands and hundreds of thousands attacking one another in open battle or in mile long trench warfare, this exchange of shots between two buildings across a Dublin green may seem petty. But to us there could be nothing greater. Every shot we fired was a declaration to the world that Ireland, a small country but large in our hearts, was demanding her independence. We knew that all over Dublin, perhaps by this time all over Ireland, other groups like ours were filled with the same intensity, the same determination, to make the Irish Republic, no matter how short-lived, a reality of which history would have to take account. Besides, the longer we could keep our tricolour flying over the College of Surgeons, the greater the chance that Irish courage would respond and we should gain recruits.

Whenever I was called down to carry a dispatch I took off my uniform, put on my grey dress and hat and went out the side door of the college with my message. As soon as I returned, I slipped back into my uniform and joined the firing squad.

There were a good many of the *Fianna* boys in the college with us. As usual, their allegiance to Madam would not let them leave her. One of them, Tommy Keenan of Camden Row, was only 12 years old, but was invaluable. He would go out for food and medicine and, because he was so little, never attracted attention, though he wore his green *Fianna* shirt under his jacket. On Tuesday he came to the conclusion, perhaps with Madam's aid, that he ought to go home and tell his parents what he was doing. Commandant Mallin advised him, just before he left, to take off his green shirt and not wear it again for a while. It was a day or more before he returned, because his father had locked him in his room. We sympathised with the father, for that was just what we had expected him to do. But when a friend came along who promised to keep guard over Tommy if he was allowed to go for a walk, the boy's chance came. Eluding this friend, he ran the most roundabout way until he arrived where he felt 'duty' called him.[21]

The boy already referred to as nearly blind was with us, too. He pleaded so hard to be allowed to use a rifle that the men finally put him at a loophole, where he breathlessly fired shot after shot in the direction of the hotel. Maybe the prayers he murmured gave him success.

Our rations were short, but I do not remember that anyone complained. I for one had no appetite for more than a slice of bread or two a day, with a cup of bouillon made from the cubes laid in as part of our necessary ration. The two captured British officers had their meals regularly whether anyone else ate or not and seemed grateful for it.

Every evening fighting would quiet down and the boys and men – about a hundred, now, through recruits who had joined us – would gather in the largest lecture hall to sing under the leadership of Jo Connolly, whose brother Sean had fallen the first day in front of Dublin Castle. I can hear them even now:

Armed for the battle.
Kneel we before Thee,
Bless Thou our banners,

---

21. At 13 years old Tommy Keenan was the youngest participant in the Rising and is on the St Stephen's Green Roll of Honour. He would go on to fight in the Irish War of Independence and the Irish Civil War.

God of the brave!
Ireland is living –
Shout we triumphant,
Ireland is waking –
Hands grasp the sword!

They were singing this chant, written by the countess and set to some Polish revolutionary air, on Wednesday evening. I was upstairs, studying a map of our surroundings and trying to find a way by which we could dislodge the soldiers from the roof of the Hotel Shelbourne. When Commandant Mallin came in, I asked him if he would let me go out with one man and try to throw a bomb attached to an eight second fuse through the hotel window. I knew there was a bow window on the side farthest from us which was not likely to be guarded. We could use our bicycles and get away before the bomb exploded – that is, if we were quick enough. At any rate, it was worth trying, whatever the risk.

Commandant Mallin agreed the plan was a good one, but much too dangerous. I pointed out to him that it had been my speed which had saved me so far from machine gun fire on the hotel roof. It was not that the British were doing us any real harm in the college, but it was high time to take the aggressive, for success would hearten the men in other 'forts' who were not having as safe a time of it. He finally agreed, though not at all willingly, for he did not want to let a woman run this sort of risk.

My answer to that argument was that we had the same right to risk our lives as the men; that in the constitution of the Irish Republic, women were on an equality with men. For the first time in history, indeed, a constitution had been written that incorporated the principle of equal suffrage. But the Commandant told me there was another task to be accomplished before the hotel could be bombed. That was to cut off the retreat of a British force which had planted a machine gun on the flat roof of University Church. It was against our rules to use any church, Protestant or Catholic, in our defence, no matter what advantage that might give us. But this church, close at hand, had been occupied by the British and was cutting us off from another command with whom it was necessary to keep in communication. In order to cut off the retreat of these soldiers, it would be necessary to burn two buildings. I asked the Commandant to let me help in this undertaking. He consented and gave me four men to help fire one building, while another party went out to fire the other. It meant a great deal to me that he should trust me with this piece of work and I felt elated. While I changed once more into my uniform, for the work of war can only be done by those who wear its dress, I could still hear them singing:

> Who fights for Ireland,
> God guide his blows home,
> Who dies for Ireland,
> God give him peace!
> Knowing our cause just,
> March we victorious,
> Giving our hearts' blood
> Ireland to free!

9

IT TOOK ONLY a few moments to reach the building we were to set afire. Councillor Partridge smashed the glass door in the front of a shop that occupied the ground floor. He did it with the butt of his rifle and a flash followed. It had been discharged! I rushed past him into the doorway of the shop, calling to the others to come on. Behind me came the sound of a volley and I fell. It was as I had on the instant divined. That flash had revealed us to the enemy.

'It's all over,' I muttered as I felt myself falling. But a moment later when I knew I was not dead I was sure I should pull through. Before another volley could be fired, Mr Partridge lifted and carried me into the street. There on the sidewalk lay a dark figure in a pool of blood. It was Fred Ryan, a mere lad of 17, who had wanted to come with us as one of the party of four. 'We must take him along,' I said. But it was no use; he was dead.

With help, I managed to walk to the corner. Then the other man who had stopped behind to set the building afire caught up with us. Between them they succeeded in carrying me back to the College of Surgeons.

As we came into the vestibule, Jo Connolly was

waiting with his bicycle, ready to go out with me to bomb the hotel.

His surprise at seeing me hurt was as if I had been out for a stroll upon peaceful streets and met with an accident.

They laid me on a large table and cut away the coat of my fine, new uniform. I cried over that. Then they found I had been shot in three places, my right side under the arm, my right arm and in the back on my right side. Had I not turned as I went through that shop door to call to the others, I would have got all three bullets in my back and lungs and surely been done for.

They had to probe several times to get the bullets, and all the while Madam held my hand. But the probing did not hurt as much as she expected it would. My disappointment at not being able to bomb the Hotel Shelbourne was what made me unhappy. They wanted to send me to the hospital across the Green, but I absolutely refused to go. So the men brought in a cot and the first aid girls bandaged me, as there was no getting a doctor that night. What really did distress me was my cough and the pain in my chest. When I tried to keep from coughing, I made a queer noise in my throat and noticed everyone around me look frightened.

'It's no death rattle,' I explained, and they all had to laugh – that is, all laughed except Commandant Mallin. He said he could not forgive himself as long as he lived for having let me go out on that errand. But he did not live long, poor fellow! I tried to cheer him by pointing out that he had in reality saved my life, since the bombing plan was much more dangerous.

Soon after I was brought in, the countess and Councillor Partridge disappeared. When she returned to me, she said very quietly, 'You are avenged, my dear.'

It seems they had gone out to where Fred Ryan lay, and Partridge, to attract the fire of the soldiers across the street in the *Sinn Fein* Bank, had stooped over the dead boy to lift him. There were only two soldiers and they both fired. That gave Madam a chance to sight them. She fired twice and killed both.

They tell me that all next day I was delirious and lay moaning and talking incoherently. It was not the bullets that brought me to this pass, but pneumonia. Even so I am glad I was there and not at a hospital. Later a doctor who was summoned made the mistake of using too much corrosive sublimate on my wounds, and for once I knew what torture is. The mistake took all the skin off my side and back. But Madam is a natural nurse. Among her friends she was noted for her desire to care for them if they fell ill. Someone was almost always in bed at Surrey House; some friend whose eyes might be troubling her to whom the countess would read aloud or apply soothing applications; a *Fianna* boy, or an actress from the Abbey Theatre who needed to build up her nerves. Thus I was in good hands, and besides, following my instinct, I ate nothing for the next three days but drank quantities of water.

Once a day they allowed me visitors. Everyone who came to my room was confident that things were going well. That we were isolated from other 'forts' and even from headquarters did not necessarily mean they were losing ground. We were holding out, and our spirits rose high. We believed, too, that by this time the Volunteers outside Dublin had risen. We could not know that, even where they had joined the Rising on Easter Monday, the loss of one day had given the British enough time to be on guard, so that in no instance could our men enter the barracks and seize arms as originally planned.

While I lay there I could hear the booming of big guns. All of us believed it was the Germans attacking the British on the water. There had been a rumour that German submarines would come into the fight if they learned there was a chance of our winning it. I had heard that report the evening before the Rising. Edmond Kent,[22] one of the republican leaders, had been most confident of our success and when a friend asked him, 'What if the British bring up their big guns?' he replied, 'The moment they bring up their big guns, we win.'

He did not explain what he meant by this, but I took it that he expected outside aid the minute the British, recognising our revolt as serious, gave us the dignity of combatants by using heavy artillery against us. Whatever he meant, the fact remains that when they took this action, they made us a 'belligerent' in the world's eyes and gave us the excuse we could so well use – an appeal to the world court as a 'small nation', for a place at the coming peace conference.

Sunday morning one of the dispatch girls, white and scared because she had been escorted to our 'fort' by British soldiers, came from headquarters to inform Commandant Mallin that a general surrender had been decided on. The Commandant and Madam were in my

---

22. Eamonn Ceannt, one of the seven signatories of the Proclamation of the Irish Republic, executed 8 May 1916.

room at the time and Madam instantly grew pale.

'Surrender?' she cried. 'We'll never surrender!'

Then she begged the Commandant, who could make the decision for our division, not to think of giving in. It would be better, she said, for all of us to be killed at our posts. I felt as she did about it, but the girl who had brought the dispatch became more and more excited, saying that the soldiers outside had threatened to 'blow her little head off' if she did not come out soon with the word they wanted. Possibly they suspected any Irish girl would be more likely to urge resistance than surrender.

Commandant Mallin, to quiet us I suppose, said he would not surrender unless forced to do so.[23] But he must have decided to give in at once, for in less than an hour an ambulance came to take me to St Vincent's Hospital, just across the Green. As they carried me downstairs, our boys came out to shake my hand. I urged them again and again to hold out. As I said goodbye to Commandant Mallin I had a feeling I should never see him again. Not that it entered my head for a moment that he would be executed by the British. Despite all our wrongs and their injustices, I did not dream of their killing prisoners of war.

I felt no such dread concerning the countess, though our last words together were about her will. I had witnessed it and she had slipped it in the lining of my coat. I was to get it to her family at the earliest possible moment. It was fortunate that I did.

23. Commandant Mallin did not immediately respond to the surrender order brought by Nurse Elizabeth Farrell, instead St Stephen's Green was one of the last outposts to surrender and then only because the order was countersigned by James Connolly.

My departure was the first move in the surrender. That afternoon all the revolutionists gave up their arms to the British in St Patrick's Square.

10

THOSE FIRST TWO weeks in St Vincent's Hospital were the blackest of my life. In that small, white room I was, at first, as much cut off as though in my grave. I had a fever and the doctors and nurses were more worried over my pneumonia than over my wounds, though every time they dressed them I suffered from the original treatment with corrosive sublimate. My greatest anxiety, however, was because I could get no word to my mother in Glasgow. I knew she would think I had been killed.

That was just what happened. The first word she had received since the day I left home was that I was dead; that I had been shot in the spine and left lying on the Dublin pavement for two days. The next rumour that reached her was that I was not dead, but paralyzed. The third report was that the British had sentenced me to 15 years' imprisonment. Had I not been wounded, the last would probably have been true. After two weeks I wrote a letter and the doctor had it forwarded home for me. It had not been easy work writing it, for my right arm was the one that had been wounded. I knew, though, that unless she had word in my own handwriting, my mother might not believe what she read.

Presently news began to drift in to me of trials and executions. I could not get it through my head. Why were these men not treated as prisoners of war? We had obeyed all rules of war and surrendered as formally as any army ever capitulated. All my reports were of death; nothing but death!

At dawn on 3 May the British shot Pádraig Pearse, Thomas MacDonagh and old Tom Clarke. The following day they shot Joseph Plunkett, the brother of Pádraig Pearse[24] and two other leaders, Daly and O'Hanrahan.

The third day John McBride, a man known the world over for his stand in the Boer War, was shot to death. He was the only one killed that day and we wondered why. What was this British reasoning that determined who should go in company with his fellows and who should go alone?

At length came the turn of the Countess Markievicz. Because she was a woman, they commuted her death sentence to penal servitude for life. I was very glad; but I knew that, since she had fought as one of them, she would rather have died with them. Penal servitude! Those words rang like a knell for one who was all energy, who needed people around her, who wanted to serve.

The British did not shoot anyone on Sunday. They let us meditate on all that the past week had done to our leaders. There is no torture so excruciating as suspense. It is the suspense which Ireland has had to endure for generations that has weakened her more than any battles. How we have waited and waited! It has

---

24. Willie Pearse.

always been hard for us to believe we were not to realise our hopes. Even in these latter years during which Home Rule has loomed large before us, we have not suspected that, in the end, it would become only a parliamentary trick and a delusion. If anyone had told me the Sunday before that all these men were to be shot, I should not have believed them. Our bitter belief has been forced upon us.

On Monday the British began it again. This time it was Michael Mallin they stood against a wall and shot. I remembered how, when I was so ill at the College of Surgeons, he had been gentle with me. He always had tried to ease the discomforts of his men. You would never have guessed by looking at him, he was so quiet and restrained, that he had been waiting 20 years for the day which would make him a commandant over Irish soldiers. He told me that, as a boy of 14, he had enlisted in the British army to get experience with which to fight Great Britain. When he was stationed in India, he said, he had lain awake night after night, planning how some day he could put his military knowledge at Ireland's service. Six days he served Ireland; eight days he lay in prison; now he was dead.

Later his widow came to see me. She brought me the notebook he used when writing the dispatches I carried. She brought me, besides, some small bits of Irish poplin he had woven himself. She did not break down; she seemed exalted. It was the same with all the wives of those shot and with the mother of Pádraic and William Pearse. You would have thought they had been greatly honoured, that their dignity was equal to bearing it.

Yet they all had terrible stories of cruelty to tell me. Kilmainham Prison was a grim waiting room for death. In addition, the court-martial never lasted long enough for anyone to feel he had been fairly tried and judged. I heard all the prison sentences, over a hundred that first week! Most of them were for long terms and five for life. Councillor Partridge was given a 15 year sentence that afterward was commuted to ten.

It is not the same thing to read of executions and sentences in the press and to hear of them from the lips of friends – the wives, mothers and daughters of the men executed or sentenced for life. To feel we had failed in our purpose was enough to make us brood; but to know that never again would these men sing rebel songs together or tell of their hopes...

At length Nora Connolly and her sister came to see me. They told me of their father's last hours; how, because of his wound that already had brought him close to death, he had to be strapped into a chair to face the firing squad. I thought of gentle Mrs Connolly saying goodbye to her husband, knowing all the while what was about to take place.

Some of the first aid girls who had been in prison for 15 days came to visit me, too. We compared notes. I learned then how Chris Caffrey had been stripped and searched by British soldiers to her shame, for she was a modest girl. But she had eaten her dispatch before they dragged her off the street where she had been bicycling. I heard, too, how Chris had been almost prevented from reaching headquarters by a crowd of poor women gathered about the Post Office for their usual weekly 'separation allowance'. Their husbands were all fighting in France or Flanders for the British. They would not get their allowance this week and were terror stricken, crowding about the Post Office and crying and shouting hysterically. Chris, as we called Christine, had to fire her revolver at the ground before they would make way for her.

Next followed the story of Francis Sheehy Skeffington, one of the few men in Dublin we could go to for advice about the law when we had any plan to carry out. He had been shot without a trial, they said; without even knowing, when called out into the little courtyard, that he was about to be killed. And he had had nothing to do with the Rising! He always had been against the use of force. When he was arrested, after a day spent in trying to get a committee of safety together because the police had disappeared, his wife did not even know where he was. She had no word of his death until a day after he was buried in quicklime, the burial of a criminal.

Ah, how the stories of Belgian atrocities which we had heard from the lips of the Archbishop of Michelin when the Great War broke out paled beside this one fortnight in Dublin! We did not know when it would end or how. There ensued a reign of terror in all Irish homes, whether the men or women had had anything to do with the Rising or not. For both soldiers and police were now given power to arrest anyone they pleased. Several hundred men were put in prison under no charge, nor were any charges ever preferred in many cases.

The women, too! Helena Molony and Dr Katherine Lynn, whose motor Madam had used that night in St

Stephen's Green and whose bicycle I had been riding, were both arrested Easter Monday and taken to Dublin Castle. Miss Molony was discovered a few hours later with the lock half off her door, her fingers bleeding pitifully from attempts to get out.[25] Next they were taken to Kilmainham jail, where for 15 days those two women, with 80 others, were kept in a room completely lacking any sanitary arrangements. We used to shudder at stories of such deeds, which we then believed could happen only in Siberia. Dr Lynn is famous for her surgical skill. She is one of the Irish doctors to whom the British send their worst war cripples for treatment and is far more successful than them in treating such cases. Many visitors to Dublin have seen Miss Molony on the stage of the Abbey Theatre and recognised her talent. Dr Lynn was deported to Bath; Miss Molony was sent to the Aylesbury Prison and kept there a year.[26] Never once during that time was any charge preferred against her.

Little Tommy Keenan of Camden Row had, so he thought, the good fortune to be put in prison with 60 of the *Fianna* when our men surrendered the College of Surgeons. But, much to their chagrin, at the end of two weeks the boys were released. Did they scurry away to grow up into better British subjects? Not at all! Tommy lined them up in front of the jail and led them off down the street singing 'The Watch on the Rhine' at the top of their lungs.

---

25. Helena Molony later tried to dig her way out of Kilmainham Gaol with a spoon.
26. There, Molony continued to cause difficulties for the authorities by publicising the terrible conditions through her connections with the Workers' Suffrage Federation.

There was no end to the stories I heard as I lay there in the hospital. Stories of heroism and stories of disaster followed one another, each strengthening my belief that the courage and honour of the heroic days of Ireland were still alive in our hearts. Perhaps it is for this we should love our enemies: when they cleave with their swords the heart of a brave man, they lay bare the truth of life.

11

THERE CAME A day when I could no longer endure lying alone in my room thinking of all that had happened for this reason or that. The nurses had been very kind to me. Some of them were in sympathy with the *Sinn Féin* movement, while all of them felt the horror of the executions. There were times when I could rise above this horror and cheer them, too, by singing a rebel song. I had interested them, besides, in suffrage work we had been doing in Glasgow, where for several years 1,100 militants had done picketing and the like.

Finally, however, I persuaded them to let me move into the public ward, where I could see other women patients and talk a little. There were about 20 women and girls in the ward. Nine of them, who had nothing to do with the Rising, had been wounded by British soldiers. The nurses insisted this was accidental. But the women themselves would not agree to that explanation, nor did I, for I recalled the Red Cross girls being shot at – a thing I had seen with my own eyes. I told the nurses I had seen the British firing at our ambulances in the belief, no doubt, that we were doing what we had caught them at – transporting troops from one part of Dublin to another in ambulances. Sometimes I felt sorry to have to make those nurses see facts as they were, instead of helping them keep what few illusions still remained about their men in khaki. But I was glad when I could tell them what I had just heard of De Valera's daring.

With a handful of men, he had prevented 2,000 of the famous Sherwood Foresters coming through lower Mount Street to attack one of our positions. Or, again, it did me good to relate the story of the 17-year-old lad who singlehanded had captured a British general. The sequel to that tale, however, was not very cheerful, for the same general had sat at the court martial and gave the boy, who before had had power of life and death over him, a ten year sentence.[27]

There were three women in the ward who had all been struck by the same bullet: a mother, her daughter and a cousin. They had been friendly to the British soldiers, had fed them because, as the mother told me, her husband and son were in the trenches fighting for Great Britain. These three women had been at their window, looking with curiosity into the street, when the very soldier they had just fed turned suddenly and shot them. One had her jawbone broken, the second her arm pierced and the third was struck in the breast They were all serious wounds which kept them in bed. While I was still in the ward, the two men of this family came back from Flanders on leave, only to find no one at home. The neighbours directed them to the hospital. I hate to think how those men looked when they

---

27. This boy was likely 17-year-old John McGallogly, from Glasgow, Scotland. McGallogly took Lieutenant King of the Royal Irish Rifles prisoner and was later identified by him when court-martialled alongside Willie Pearse. McGallogly was sentenced to ten years penal servitude. The court martial lasted 15 minutes.

learned why their women wore bandages. They told me that during Easter Week the Germans put up opposite the trenches of the Irish Brigade a placard that read:

THE MILITARY ARE SHOOTING DOWN YOUR WIVES
AND CHILDREN IN DUBLIN.

But the Irish soldiers had not believed.

I asked them if it was true, as alleged, that in answer to the placard, the Irish Brigade had sung 'Rule, Britannia'. They were indignant at the idea. They might be wearing khaki, they said, but they never yet had sung 'Rule, Britannia'. When the day came for them to return to the front, the father wanted to desert, dangerous as that would be, while the son was eager to go back to the trenches.

'This time,' he said to me, 'we'll not be killing Germans!'

When rumours came later of a mutiny in the Irish regiment, I wondered to myself if these two men were at the bottom of it.

Stories of atrocities poured into our ears when the Germans invaded Belgium. Now we had to hear them from our own people and now we had to believe them. They were stories as cruel as any heard since the days of the Island Magee massacre.[28]

In the House of Commons shortly after the Rising, the cabinet was questioned if it were true that the body of a boy in the uniform of the Irish Volunteers had

---

28. Massacre of Irish Catholics by Scottish and English settlers from Carrickfergus in 1641.

been unearthed in the grounds of Trinity College, with the marks of 20 bayonet wounds upon him.

'No,' was the response, 'there were not 20; there were only 19'!

The body in question was that of Gerald Keogh, one of a family passionately devoted to the cause of Irish freedom. He had been sent to Kimmage to bring back 50 men. He went scouting ahead of them, just as I had done when I brought in the men from the Leeson Street Bridge. As he was passing Trinity College, held by the British, he was shot down and swiftly captured. It is generally understood he was asked for information and that, upon his refusing to answer, the soldiers tried to force it from him by prodding him with their bayonets. I might add that the 50 men with him were not attacked as they went by.

This boy's brother was also captured by British soldiers, who decided to hang him then and there. He begged them to shoot him, but they fastened a noose around his neck and led him to a lamp post. Fortunately an officer came along at that moment and rescued him. Even children were not safe from being terrorised by the soldiers, as Mr Dillon later brought out in the House of Commons.

There also were murders in North King Street. Fourteen men who had nothing to do with the Rising, were killed in their homes by British soldiers who buried them in their cellars, while others looted the houses. The house in Leinster Road was pillaged and the soldiers had the effrontery to sell the books, fine furniture and paintings on the street in front of the dwelling.

I had been in the hospital now about five weeks, and

had been told I might go in a few days to visit friends in the city if I would promise to return every day to have my wounds dressed. Then one morning I was informed there was a 'G-man', as we call government detectives, waiting downstairs to see me. He had been coming every day to the hospital, it seems, to learn if I was yet strong enough to go to jail. Evidently he had decided that I was, for he told me I must accompany him to Bridewell Prison.

When I went up to the ward to say goodbye and get my things I found the nurses terribly upset. You see, it brought the Irish question right home to that hospital. They went to him in a body and tried to beg me off, but he insisted on his rights, and away I went despite tears and protestations.

This was the first time I had been out, so naturally I felt queer and weak. Nor was I pleased with my companion. He had a fat, self-satisfied face; in fact, was not at all the handsome, keen looking detective you see on the cover of a dime novel. Besides, he was too polite. He thought, I suppose, that this would be the best way to get me to answer the hundred and one questions he began to ask me. I told him I might answer questions about myself, but I certainly should not answer any concerning the countess or my other friends.

This response kept him quiet for a block or two. Then he turned suddenly and asked me about two girls from Glasgow who had come to Ireland at the same time that I did. I just walked along as though I had not heard a word, and so we proceeded in silence the rest of the way.

When we entered the vestibule of the prison an old

official immediately began to catechise me. I refused to answer a single one of his questions, not even as to my name. Instead I pointed to the 'G-man'.

'Ask him,' I said. 'He knows all about me, and can tell you if he wants to.'

The detective's face grew red, but he did answer the old man's questions. It was very interesting to me to find that he knew who my parents were; that I had been born 12 miles from Glasgow; that I had gone to different schools which he named, and that I had attended the training college for teachers. He told just where I had been teaching, and how well known I was as a militant suffragette. But what he did not say was even more interesting. He never declared that I had been a combatant in the Rising. I wondered inwardly if he thought I had been only a dispatch rider or a first aid girl. I was exceedingly glad I had let him answer for me as, taking it for granted they knew all about me, I might have given myself away.

The old man finally called the matron and told her to treat me well, as I was not a 'drunk or disorderly' person, to which class this prison is given over, but a military prisoner. Indeed she did treat me well. Since there was nothing on which to sit down, she kindly opened a cell and let me sit on the wooden plank they call a bed and stare at the wooden headboard. I did not look forward much to such accommodations, with my wounds still painful. She talked to me, too, very sympathetically. Sometimes it was hard for us to hear each other, as there were many drunken men singing and cursing. Being drunk, they were able to forget that Ireland was under martial law and cursed the British loudly or sang disrespectful songs.

The detective had gone out and those in the jail seemed waiting to hear from him before they picked out my permanent cell. After about two hours, he came back. From where I sat, I could see him bend over the old man and whisper to him. Then he walked over to me.

'Come,' he said, 'we'll go now.'

'Go where?' I asked.

'To the hospital,' he replied, 'or anywhere else you wish. You are free.' The matron was as pleased as if she were a friend of mine. I was too amazed to know what to think. I told the detective, however, that as I did not know this part of Dublin I could not find my way back to the hospital without his company. Off we went again and he paid my car fare, for which I thanked him.

In the sky overhead were aeroplanes that the British kept hovering over Dublin to impress the people.

'Are those the little things with which you fight the Zeppelins?' I asked my detective.

This remark hurt his feelings. He was not British, he informed me, but a good Redmondite.[29] How embarrassed he was when I asked him if he liked arresting Irish who had shown their love of Ireland by being willing to die for her and, what sometimes seemed worse to me, going into an English prison for life. After that we did not talk any more until he said goodbye to me at the hospital door.

The nurses were not as surprised to see me back as I had expected them to be. They had known I was re-

---

29. A supporter of parliamentarian John Redmond who sought Irish Home Rule.

turning, for it was the head doctor who had telephoned the authorities at Dublin Castle to tell them, with a good deal of heat, that I was in no condition to begin a prison sentence. That must have been what the 'G-man' had whispered to the old official at Bridewell Prison.

12

AFTER TWO WEEKS more, I left the hospital and went to stay with a friend in Dublin. It seemed very strange to me not to be going back to Surrey House. How everything had changed! As soon as I was strong enough I went around to see where the fighting had destroyed whole streets. Dublin was scarred and, it seemed to me, very sick. I recalled momentarily that a teacher of mine had once said the name Dublin meant 'the Black Pool'.

The building where I had first met Thomas MacDonagh, the Volunteer headquarters, had a 'to let' sign in its windows. Who would want to engage in business in a place where such high hopes had been blasted?

Liberty Hall was a shell, empty of everything but memories.

Around the Post Office all other buildings had been levelled, but the great building stood there like a monument to Easter Week. The windows stared vacantly from the house on Leinster Road. Everything had been taken from it. The looters must have had a merry time. Hundreds of houses had been thus sacked, for the British soldiers had lived up to that Tommy whose words make Kipling's famous song:

Then the sweatin' Tommies wonder as they spade the beggars under,
Why lootin' should be entered as a crime;
So if my song you'll 'ear, I will learn you plain an' clear
'Ow to pay yourself for fightin' overtime.
With the loot!
Bloomin' loot!
That's the thing to make the boys git up and shoot!
It's the same with dogs and men,
If you'd make 'em come again
Clap 'em forward with a
Loo! Loo! Lulu!
Loot![30]

Against our soldiers, on the other hand, a great many of whom were very poor, there had not been a single accusation of looting. In the Post Office, for instance, they ordered one of the captured British officers to guard the safe. In the streets where windows had been broken, they tried to keep the people from pillaging the shops. Whatever money our men found lying loose in the buildings they occupied was turned over to their superior officers.

Again and again I myself had seen men of the Citizen Army, quite as poor as any British soldier, hand over money to Commandant Mallin. Had I only thought of it, I could have taken this with me when I was carried to the hospital. The cause would have been at least one hundred pounds richer.

At the College of Surgeons we had destroyed nothing except a portrait of Queen Victoria. We took that

---

30. Rudyard Kipling's 'Loot'.

down and made puttees out of it. We did not feel we were doing any wrong, for it was Queen Victoria who, in 1848, wrote to her uncle, King Leopold of Belgium:

> There are ample means of crushing the rebellion in Ireland and I think it very likely to go off without any contest, which people (I think rightly) rather regret. The Irish should receive a good lesson or they will begin it again.

From this quotation anyone can see that the Queen looked upon the Irish as aliens which, indeed, they are.

We also were very careful of the museum and library at the College of Surgeons. Although the men did not have any covering and the nights were cold, they did not cut up the rugs and carpets, but doubled them and crept in between the folds in rows.

About Jacob's Biscuit Factory, during Easter Week, even though it was a very dangerous spot, the employees had hovered, for fear their means of livelihood would be destroyed. But it was not. The machinery was left uninjured, for we always remembered our own poor.

At the Guinness brewery, where great quantities of stout were stored, none of it was touched. Most of our men are teetotallers, anyway.

Some of the poor of Dublin had tried to pillage at first, but it was a pathetic attempt. I saw one specimen of this on Easter Tuesday while carrying a dispatch. There was a crowd of people about a shoe shop. The windows had been smashed and the poor wretches were clambering into the shop at great risk of cutting themselves. Once inside, despite all the outer excitement, they were taking the time to try on shoes! Many of them, one could see, had never had a pair of new shoes in their lives. Visitors to Dublin going through the poorer parts are always surprised at the number of children and young girls who walk about barefooted in icy weather. It is in this way that their health is undermined.

One day during the week after I left the hospital, I heard that a batch of prisoners was to be taken to England aboard a cattle boat leaving the pier called North Wall. I went down at once to watch for them. It was a very wet day and the prisoners had been marched six miles from Richmond bar racks through the pouring rain. But they were singing their rebel songs, just as if they had never been defeated and were not on their way to the unknown horrors of an English prison.[31]

The officer in charge seemed much excited, though he had 500 soldiers to look after a hundred prisoners.

'For God's sake, close in, or we'll be rushed!' he shouted to his men. Then the soldiers, with fixed bayonets, 'closed in' upon the wet crowd of rebels, who actually seemed to feel the humour of it.

I knew some of the boys, and walked in-between the bayonets to shake hands with them and march a part of the way. They had heard I was dead, and looked at first as if they were seeing a ghost One of them, a little, lame playwright of whom I had caught a glimpse at Bridewell, had told me at the time that he was writing a farce about the revolution to show its absurdity. He

---

31. These detainees were taken to Knutsford Prison, Cheshire, England.

had had nothing to do with the Rising, for it was his brother who had been with us at the College of Surgeons. There was not even a charge against him; yet here he was, limping along in the rain and mud, but still cheerful. This chap gave me a bundle of clothes and a message for his mother, so I hunted her up the next morning. She did not know he had been deported and was in despair, for she had left her little cottage in the country to be near her son in Dublin. When I visited her she was just back from market with fruit she had bought to take to him, as it was visiting day at the barracks.

These are some of the things that made even quiet old mothers grow bitter.

13

NO ONE COULD leave Ireland for Scotland without a special permit from Dublin Castle. This permit was given only when one applied in person, so I decided to go after it. My friends were terrified; it was putting my head into the lion's mouth. But it was the only way, even though I might never come out of that building free.

I took my arm out of the sling, hoping I should not have to raise it; for I couldn't, nor can yet. For greater precaution, just before I reached Dublin Castle I removed the republican colours I always wore and put them in my pocket.

I was taken to a room where a police officer began to ask me questions. It was, I believe, my 'loyal' Scotch accent that put them off guard, when I asked for a permit to go to Glasgow.

At the hospital one of the nurses shook her head, following a long talk, and said, 'Your opinions and your accent don't go together.'

I have often been told that I look more like a teacher of mathematics, which indeed I am, than like an Irish rebel, of which I am more proud.

The officer first asked me my name. I confess that I gave it to him while wondering what his next words would be. He merely asked my address in Dublin, so I gave him the address of friends with whom I was staying. Would that disturb him, I wondered?

'When did you come to Dublin?' he next asked.

'Holy Thursday,' I replied.

'Then you've been here during the Rising?'

'Yes,' I said.

In a tone which showed how deeply he had been moved by Easter Week, he added, 'It's been a terrible business!'

To that I could feelingly agree.

At length he gave me a permit, not one to leave Dublin, but merely to see the military authorities. Here was another ordeal.

I went up to a soldier in the corridor and asked him where I should go.

'What's your name?' he asked.

'It's on this permit,' I replied, holding it out to him.

But, as he seemed afraid to touch it, I told him my name and he took me to the office where the military authorities were located. I shivered a little at the chance of his going in with me and telling them I was a rebel. But he left me at the door.

To my relief, the questions put to me here were the same as before. I had only to tell the truth and the polite officer handed over my pass.

As soon as I was outside the castle I replaced my republican colours and went home to friends who really did not expect to see me again.

I did not go directly to Glasgow, however, for I heard that the police were watching all incoming trains. Instead I went to a little seaside resort to recuperate. My sister, who had come over to Dublin to be with me after I left the hospital, went along too. She was terrified when we got off the boat because police were watching the gangway.

But nothing happened. My mother came to see me and took it all splendidly, though from the first I had given her an anxious time of it. She is a good rebel, I was proud that I could tell my mother I had been mentioned three times for bravery in dispatches sent to headquarters. The third time was when I was wounded. Commandant Mallin had said then, 'You'll surely be given the republican cross.' But the republic did not last long enough for that. I was given an Irish cross. This was the joint gift of the *Cumann na mBan* girls and the Irish Volunteers of Glasgow. They arranged, as a surprise for me, a meeting with addresses and songs. Since I had no hint of it, I was out of Scotland on the day set. They had to repeat part of the ceremony when I came back. It all was meant to be very solemn, but somehow I felt strange and absurd to be getting a cross for bravery that had led to death or prison for so many others.

I had left Scotland very quietly to go to England and see some of our boys being held in Reading Jail without any charge against them. I had had a good talk with them, even though a guard stood near all the time. He was a pleasant enough person, so we included him in our conversation, explaining the whole Rising to him. The boys were in good spirits, too. They laughed when I told them I had always boasted I would never set foot in England. And here, on their account, I was not only in England, but in an English prison.

We had very few Irish revolutionists in the Scotch prisons. Two hundred of them were brought, during August, to Barlinnie Prison, but they were allowed to stay only a short time. Far too much sympathy was expressed for them by the Irish in Glasgow and by Scotch suffragettes, who made a point of going to visit them and taking them comforts. Presently they were removed to the camp at Frongoch, Wales, where several hundred others who had taken part in the Rising were interned. As they marched through the streets of Glasgow we could not help noticing how much larger and finer looking they appeared than the British soldiers guarding them. They were men from Galway – men who for six long days had put up a memorable fight in that county, and with less than forty rifles had held six hundred square miles! Three thousand of the rifles that went down with the *Aud* had been promised to Galway. Yet five hundred men had been ready to 'go out' when they heard that, despite the countermanding order, Dublin forces were rebelling, no matter what the odds.

14

When I went back to Dublin in August, it was to find that almost everyone on the streets was wearing republican colours. The feeling was bitter, too – so bitter that the British soldiers had orders to go about in fives and sixes, but never singly. They were not allowed by their officers to leave the main thoroughfares, and had to be in barracks before dark – that is, all except the patrol. The city was still under martial law, but it seemed to me the military authorities were the really nervous persons. Much of this bitterness came from the fact that people remembered how, after the war in South Africa which lasted three years instead of five days, only one man had been executed.[32] After our Rising 16 men had been put to death.

Everywhere I heard the opinion expressed that if the revolution could have lasted a little longer, we would have been flooded with recruits. As it was, the Rising had taken people completely by surprise. Before they could recover from that surprise, it was over, and its leaders were paying the penalty of death or imprisonment. One week is a short time for the general, uninformed mass of a dominated people to decide whether an outbreak of any sort is merely an impotent rebel-

32. The Second Boer War.

lion, or a real revolution with some promise of success. Besides, there have been so many isolated protests in Ireland, doomed from the first to failure.

There was evidence everywhere that the feeling of bitterness was not vague, but the direct result of fully understanding what had happened. At a moving picture performance of *The Great Betrayal*, I was surprised at the spirit of daring in the audience. The story was about one of those abortive nationalist revolts in Italy which preceded the revolution that made Italy free. The plot was parallel in so many respects to the Easter Week Rising in Ireland that crowds flocked every day to see it. In the final picture, when the heroic leaders were shot in cold blood, men in the audience called out bitterly, 'That's right, Colthurst! Keep it up!'

Colthurst was the man who shot Sheehy Skeffington without trial on the second day of the Rising. He had been promoted for his deeds of wanton cruelty, and only the fact that a royal commission was demanded by Skeffington's widow and her friends, made it necessary to adjudge him insane as excuse for his behaviour, when that behaviour was finally brought to light.

It was on the occasion of my visit to the moving pictures that I was annoyed by the knowledge that a detective was following me. His only disguise was to don Irish tweeds such as 'Irish Irelanders' wear to stimulate home industry. He had been following me about Dublin ever since my arrival for my August visit. To this day I don't know why he did not arrest me, nor what he was waiting for me to do. But I decided now to give him the slip. In Glasgow I have had much practice jumping on cars going at full speed. The Dublin cars are much slower so as a car passed me in the middle of the block I suddenly leaped aboard, leaving my British friend standing agape with astonishment on the sidewalk. Doubtless he felt the time had come for me to carry out whatever plot I had up my sleeve, and that he had been defeated in his purpose of looking on. I never saw him again.

Even the children of Ireland have become republicans. There was a strike not long ago in Dublin schools because an order was issued by the authorities that school children should not wear republican colours. The day after the teachers made this announcement some few children obeyed the order, but they appeared in white dresses with green and orange ribbons in their hair or cap. When this, too, was forbidden, the pupils in one of the schools marched out in a body and proceeded to other schools throughout the city to call out the pupils on strike. Any school that did not obey their summons promptly had its windows smashed. Finally, the police were called and marched against them. The children, as the sympathetic press put it, 'retreated in good order to Mountjoy Square, where they took their stand and defended their position with what ammunition was at hand, namely, paving stones.' The end of it all was that the children won and went back to school wearing as many badges or flags as they wished.

Irish boys are showing their attitude, too, for at Pádraig Pearse's school, conducted now by a brother of Thomas MacDonagh who taught there before the Rising, there are several hundred boys on the waiting list. The school never was as crowded before; the work that Pearse gave his life for, the inspiriting of Irish youth, is still going on.

Out on Leinster Road one day, I walked past that house where, not nine months before, I had met so many people of the republican movement. The house was empty, with that peculiar look of bereavement that some houses wear. It had been an embodiment of the Countess Markievicz and, now that she was gone, looked doomed. Where was she? Over in England in Aylesbury Prison, but fortunately at work in the kitchen. I could not fancy her depressed beyond activity of some sort that in the end would be for Ireland's good.

'A felon's cap's the noblest crown an Irish head can wear.'[33]

This was one of her favourite quotations, and I knew that in wearing the cap, her courage would not desert her. Her sister had seen her, and told me she was in good spirits; grateful that they had put her to work and not left her to inactivity or brooding thoughts. She had repeated what an old woman in Mountjoy Prison had said to her: 'Man never built a wall but God Almighty threw a gap in it!'

Last November I paid another visit to Dublin. The bitterness had increased.

Here is one of my favourite songs as a child:

---

33. This line was inscribed on the medal presented to James Connolly by the Independent Labour Party of Ireland for his part in the 'Dublin Labour War 1913–1914'. 'The Felons of Our Land' is a favourite old Irish rebel song of Margaret's which she included in this volume.

O'Donnell Aboo

Proudly the note of the trumpet is sounding,
Loudly the war cries arise on the gale;
Fleetly the steed by Lough Swilly is bounding,
To join the thick squadrons in Saimear's green vale.
On, every mountaineer,
Strangers to flight and fear!
Rush to the standard of dauntless Red Hugh!
Bonnaught and Gallowglass,
Throng from each mountain pass;
Onward for Erin, O'Donnell Aboo!

Princely O'Neill to our aid is advancing
With many a chieftain and warrior clan.
A thousand proud steeds in his vanguard are prancing
Neath borderers brave from the Banks of the Bann.
Many a heart shall quail
Under its coat of mail;
Deeply the merciless foeman shall rue,
When on his ear shall ring,
Borne on the breezes' wing,
Tir Chonaill's dread war-cry, 'O'Donnell Aboo!'

Wildly o'er Desmond the war wolf is howling!
Fearless the eagle sweeps over the plain!
The fox in the streets of the city is prowling!
All who would scare them are banished or slain!
Grasp every stalwart hand
Hackbut and battle brand,
Pay them all back the deep debt so long due!
Norris and Clifford well

Can of Tirconnell tell;
Onward to glory, 'O'Donnell Aboo!'
Sacred the cause of Clan Chonnaill's defending,
The altars we kneel at, the homes of our sires.
Ruthless the ruin the foe is extending.
Midnight is red with the plunderers' fires.
On with O'Donnell, then!
Fight the old fight again,
Sons of Tir Chonaill, all valiant and true;
Make the false Saxon feel
Erin's avenging steel!
Strike for your country, 'O'Donnell Aboo!'

This was the other:

The Jackets Green

When I was a maiden fair and young
On the pleasant banks of Lee,
No bird that in the wild wood sang
Was half so blythe and free;
My heart ne'er beats with flying feet,
Tho' Love sand me his queen,
Till down the glen rode Saisfield's men
And they wore their jackets green.
Young Donal sat on his gallant gray
Like a king on a royal seat,
And my heart leaped out on his regal way
To worship at his feet;
Love, had you come in those colours dressed,
And woo'd with a soldier's mien,
I'd have laid my head on your throbbing breast
For the sake of the Irish green.

No hoarded wealth did my love own
Save the good sword that he bore.
But I loved him for himself alone
And the colours bright he wore.
For had he come in England's red
To make me England's queen,
I'd rove the high green hills instead
For the sake of the Irish green.
When William stormed with shot and shell
At the walls of Garryowen,
In the breach of death my Donal fell,
And he sleeps near the treaty stone.
That breach the foeman never crossed
While he swung his broadsword keen,
But I do not weep my darling lost,
For he fell in his jacket green.

Here is a song that Madam liked very much. It was the most popular song of the Fenians:

The Felons of our Land

Fill up once more, we'll drink a toast
To comrades far away,
No nation upon earth can boast
Of braver hearts than they;
And though they sleep in dungeons deep,
Or flee, outlawed and banned,
We love them yet, we can't forget
The felons of our land.
In boyhood's bloom and manhood's pride
Foredoomed by alien laws.
Some on the scaffold proudly died

For Ireland's holy cause;
And, brother, say, shall we today
Unmoved, like cowards stand,
While traitors shame and foes defame
The felons of our land?
Some in the convict's dreary cell
Have found a living tomb,
And some, unknown, unfriended, fell
Within the prison's gloom;
But what care we, although it be
Trod by a ruffian band?
God bless the clay where rest today
The felons of our land!
Let cowards sneer and tyrants frown,
Oh, little do we care!
The felon's cap's the noblest crown
An Irish head can wear!
And every Gael in Innisfail
Who scorns the serf's vile brand,
From Lee to Boyne would gladly join
The felons of our land!

This is one of the songs of earlier risings which we all sang during the last one:

Wrap the Green Flag Round Me, Boys

Wrap the green flag 'round me, boys,
To die 't were far more sweet,
With Erin's noble emblem, boys.
To be my winding sheet;
In life I longed to see it wave.
And followed where it led,

But now my eyes grow dim, my hand
Would grasp its last bright shred.
Oh, I had hopes to meet you, boys,
On many a well fought field,
When to our bright green banner, boys,
The treacherous foe would yield;
But now, alas, I am denied
My dearest earthly prayer,
You'll follow and you'll meet the foe
But I shall not be there.
But though my body molders, boys.
My spirit will be free,
And every comrade's honour, boys,
Will still be dear to me;
And in the thick and bloody fight.
Let not your courage lag,
For I 'll be there, and hovering near
Around the dear old flag!

This song, written by the Countess Markiewicz to the tune of 'The Young May Moon', had a great effect in Dublin, before the Rising, in preventing the British from getting Irish recruits. It was sung everywhere:

Antirecruiting Song

The recruiters are raidin' old Dublin, boys,
It's them we 'll have to be troublin', boys.
We'll go to their meetings and give them such greetings,
We'll give them in German for fun, me boys;
'Tis the Germans they're out to destroy, me boys,
Whose prosperity did so annoy, me boys,

So let each Irish blade just stick to his trade
And let Bull do his own dirty work, me boys.

Chorus

For the Germans are winning the war, me boys,
And England is feeling so sore, me boys.
They're passing conscription, the only prescription
To make Englishmen go to the front, me boys.
Your boss, he won't go to the war, me boys,

Hun bullets do him so annoy, me boys,
So kindly he frees you, he does it to squeeze you
To fight for his money and him, me boys;
They've hunger conscription in Ireland, boys,
You'll starve till you're thin as a wire, me boys.
You'll get very thin, but you won't care a pin
For you'll know it's for Ireland's sake, me boys.

Chorus

For the English are losing the war, me boys,
And they want us all killed before, me boys,
The great German nation has sworn their damnation,
And we'll echo the curse with a will, me boys.
Then hurrah for the gallant old Dublin, boys,
And if you wouldn't be muddlin', boys,
Join a Volunteer corps, or, if that is a bore.
The Citizen Army's as good, me boys.
Then hurrah for the Volunteers, me boys,
Ireland in arms has no fears, me boys,
And surely if we would see Ireland free.
We'll arm and we'll drill for the
Day, me boys.

Chorus

For the Germans are going to win, me boys,
And Ireland will have to butt in, me boys,
From a Gael with a gun the Briton will run,
And we'll dance at the wake of the Empire, boys!

Here is another satirical song, very popular just before and during the Rising. The man who sung it, called Brian na Banba, was deported by the English after the Rising:

Harp or Lion?

Neighbours, list and hear from me
The wondrous news I've read today,
Ireland's love of liberty
'Tis said is dead and passed away;
Irish men have all grown wiser.
Now they'll heed no ill adviser,
They despise their country's story.
All they love is England's glory –
Ha, ha, ha! Ha, ha, ha!
All they love is England's glory,
Ha, ha, ha!
Now we all must grieve to know
The deep offense our fathers gave,
Meeting men with thrust and blow
That came to rob them and enslave;
We should blush for their ill doing,
Give their errors no renewing,
And, unlike those old transgressors.
Never hurt our isle's oppressors –
Ha, ha, ha! Ha, ha, ha!

Never hurt our isle's oppressors.
Ha, ha, ha!
Only think of Hugh O'Neill,
Thundering down in furious style.
To assail with lead and steel
The rovers from our sister isle;
Chiefs and clans in all directions
With their far and near connections,
Warriors bold and swift uprisers.
Rushing on their civilisers –
Ha, ha, ha! Ha, ha, ha!
On their gracious civilisers,
Ha, ha, ha!
Surely, friends, the chance is great
We 'll cast a cloud on Emmet's fame.
Scoff at Tone and '98,
And scorn Lord Edward's honoured name;
Then, in quite a loyal manner,
Clip and dye our old green banner.
And. where hangs the harp of Brian,
Place the mangy British lion –
Ha, ha, ha! Ha, ha, ha!
Place the mangy British lion.
Ha, ha, ha!
Surely, friends, it seems to me,
England's self-ere now should know.
These are things she'll never see,
Let Ireland's star be high or low;
That's the truth, whoever denies it,
Scouts it, flouts it, or decries it,
Aids to spread a vile invention.
Drawn from – where I will not mention!

Ha, ha, ha! Ha, ha, ha!
From the place 'tis wrong to mention,
Ha, ha, ha!

Another song, written to discourage recruiting for the English army in Ireland, goes thus:

Eight Millions of Englishmen

Good old Britain, rule the waves
And gobble up all the land,
Bring out the blacks and Indian braves
To jigger the German band;
Call up Australia and Canada, too.
To shatter the Kaiser's den,
We'll stick to the looms while the howitzer booms.
Eight millions of English men;
Of mafficking, manly men;
Of valiant, loyal men;
We'll capture the trade from here to Belgrade,
Eight millions of English men.

There are plenty of fools in Ireland still,
Just promise them something soon,
A Union Jack, or a Home Rule Bill,
Or a slice of the next new moon;
And they'll rush to the colours with wild hurroos,
What price the War Lord then?
They'll settle his hash, while we gobble his cash.
Eight millions of English men;
Of beef eating, bulldog men;
Of undersized, able men;
We're shy of the guns, but we'll beggar the Huns,
Eight millions of English men.

This is a song that includes the Irish leaders in Parliament in its satire on Irish 'loyalty' to England:

> 'Now,' says Lady Aberdeen,
> 'I've a message from the Queen
> To the loyal hearts in Ireland here at home;
> She wants you all to gather socks,
> Plain as I, or decked with clocks,
> Just to prove the Irish loyal to the throne.'
>
> Chorus
>
> To Hell with the King, and God save Ireland,
> Get a sack and start the work today.
> Gather all the socks you meet, for the
> English Tommies' feet,
> When they're running from the Germans far away!
>
> 'When you've gathered all the socks,
> Send them on to Dr Cox,
> Or to Redmond, or to Dillon, or myself,
> For the party on the floor
> Have agreed to look them o'er
> While the Home Rule Bill is resting on
> the shelf.'
>
> Chorus
>
> (Same as first stanza. The first line is a parody on the loyalist toast: 'Here's a health to the King, and God save Ireland!')

The Irish Citizen Army song was written by Jo Connolly, a young working man, whose brother, Sean Connolly, was killed while leading the attack on Dublin Castle

Easter Monday. Jo was the boy who cut loopholes in the roof of the College of Surgeons. He was deported to Wandsworth Prison, but after a few months was released. The song is sung to the tune which you know as 'John Brown's Body':

The Irish Citizen Army

The Irish Citizen Army is the name of our wee band,
With our marchin' and our drillin', I'm
sure you'll call it grand;
And when we start our fightin' it will be for Ireland,
And we'll still keep marching on!

Chorus

Glory, glory to old Ireland!
Glory, glory to our Ireland!
Glory to the memory of those who
fought and fell,
And we'll still keep marching on!

We've got guns and ammunition, we
know how to use them well,
And when we meet the Saxon, we will
drive them all to Hell;
We've got to free our country and
avenge all those who fell,
So we still keep marching on!

Chorus

King George he is a coward, that no one can deny,
When the Germans come to England,
from there he'll have to fly;

And if he comes to Ireland then, by God,
he'll have to die.
And we'll still go marching on!

Chorus

When the Germans come to free us, we
will lend a helping hand,
For we believe they're just as good as any in the land.
They're bound to win our rights for us,
let England go be damned!
And we'll still keep marching on!

Here is the song of the Irish Volunteers, sung at all concerts held before the Rising to get funds for rifles and ammunition. [Now called 'A Soldier's Song' this became Ireland's national anthem in 1926 after unofficial use for several years.] The Volunteers sang it whenever they marched, and I have been told the men in the Rising also sang it. It was sung everywhere during the last Rising. When we first withdrew to the College of Surgeons, Frank Robins sang it, and we all joined in the chorus:

Volunteer Marching Song

I'll sing you a song, a soldier's song,
With a cheering, rousing chorus.
As round the blazing campfire we throng,
The starry heavens over us;
Impatient for the coming fight,
And, as we watch the dawning light,
Here in the silence of the night
We'll chant the soldier's song:

Chorus
Soldiers are we whose lives are pledged to Ireland!
Some have come from a land beyond the wave.
Sworn to be free! No more our ancient Ireland
Shall shelter the despot and the slave!
Tonight we'll man the bearna booig hill[34],
In Erin's cause come woe or weal,
Mid cannon's roar or rifle's peal,
We'll chant a soldier's song !

Mid valleys green and towering crag,
Our fathers fought before us,
And conquered 'neath the same old flag
That's proudly floating o'er us;
We're children of a fighting race
That never yet has known disgrace,
And as we go our foe to face,
We'll chant a soldier's song:

Chorus

Sons of the Gael, men of the Pale,
The long watched day is breaking!
The serried ranks of Innisfail
Have set the tyrant quaking!
But now our campfire's burning low.
See in the east a silver glow!
Out yonder waits the Saxon foe!
Then chant a soldier's song:

Chorus

---

34. Pronounced 'barnabweel,' which means, 'gap of danger.' [Margaret's note]

The *Fianna* also had their songs. One of them, written by one of the *Fianna* boys, goes:

> Draw the sword ye Irish men!
> The sword is mightier than the pen!
> Fight the good old fight again
> To crush the old transgressor!
> Break the bonds of slavery!
> O great God, it cannot be
> That Gaels could ever bend the knee
> To England, their oppressor!

Almost before it was over, the Rising became part of the great patriotic tradition of Ireland, and on all sides new songs were heard celebrating it and those who took leading parts in it. Some of these songs were heavy with a sense of the nation's tragedy. Others – those written by men who had taken part in the Rising – were often full of wit, that dauntless Irish spirit that does not forsake men even in defeat and imprisonment.

Here is a song written by a member of the Irish Republican army while he was confined in Richmond Barracks, Dublin, a month after the Rising. It is sung to the tune of 'The Mountains of Mourne':

> In Dublin's fair city there's sorrow today
> For the flower of her manhood who fell in the fray;
> Her youths and her maidens, her joy and her pride
> Have gone down in battle, in war's raging tide.
>
> They came forth to fight for a cause that was grand,
> When freedom and liberty called to their land;
> In the ardour of youth, in the spring of the year,
> They came without falter, they fought without fear.

Near the noon of that day on that April morn,
Their tramp shook the street where young Emmet was born;
They waved high their banner, white, orange and green.
And it waved over freemen, the men of '16!

And high over the Liffey it waved in the wind,
Over hearts that were brave and the noblest of minds;
And they fought as of old, and they held the old town
Till their banner, unsullied, in darkness went down.

In that Easter Week, dear old Dublin was freed,
By the blood of her sons from Swords to the Sea,
Oh, proudly again does she raise her old head
When the nations lament and salute her bold dead!

O Irish Republic! O dream of our dreams!
Resplendent in vision thy bright beauty gleams!
Though fallen and crushed 'neath thy enemy's heel,
Thy glory and beauty shine burnished like steel!

Not in vain was their death who for Ireland died,
And their deeds in our hearts in gold are inscribed;
The freeing of Ireland to us is their trust,
And we can if we will it, we can if we must!

In Dublin's fair city there's sorrow to day.
For the flower of her manhood who fell in the fray;
But in hearts that are true there is nothing of gloom,
And Erin regenerate shall rise from the tomb!

The Rising inspired not only verse, but music. One of the most popular songs in Ireland today is 'Easter Week'; the words by Francis Grenade, the music by Joseph Mary Crofts:

> Long, long the years thy chains have bound thee, Eire,
> Bitter the tears that sparkled in thy eyes,
> Sudden the cry of freedom thrills the city,
> Brave hearts beat high, thy children round thee rise;
> 'Mid shot and shell, where flaming cannon thunder.
> From out that hell we hear their battle cry:
> '*Sinn Féin Amain*!' Thy sons salute thee, Eire!
> See! Freedom's dawn is flushing in the skies!
>
> Dark Rosaleen, thy trampled flag, we swear it,
> Shall lift its sheen triumphant in the sun!
> Thy galling chain, our gallant sword shall save her,
> Ended thy pain and weeping, dearest one!
> In plaintive strains our hearts shall mourn our heroes.
> Till once again thy banner waveth free.
> Close to thy breast, then guard them, gentle Eire,
> There shall they rest till time shall cease to be!

If any proof were needed of the unbroken spirit of our men after the Rising, there could be none better than in the gay and challenging tone of many of the songs written and sung at the internment camp at Frongoch, Wales. The British guards were particularly irritated by one in which every verse ended with the line: *Sinn Féiners*, Pro Germans, alive, alive O!

But there was another that the guards not only tolerated but took to singing themselves, much to the amusement of our men. The reason they sang it was because the air was catchy and they had no means of knowing that the 'NDU' is the North Dublin Union or work house. It was written by Jack MacDonagh, brother of Thomas MacDonagh, the poet, who signed the proclamation of the republic and was shot for it.

Here is the chorus:

> Come along and join the British Army,
> Show that you're not afraid,
> Put your name upon the roll of honour,
> In the Dublin 'Pals' Brigade'!
> They'll send you out to France or Flanders,
> To show that you're true blue.
> But when the war is over.
> They won't need you anymore.
> So they'll shut you in the NDU!

Suggested Further Reading

Lorcan Collins, *16 Lives: James Connolly* (Dublin: The O'Brien Press, 2013)

Nora Connolly, *The Unbroken Tradition* (Edinburgh: Luath Press, 2016)

Brian Hughes, *16 Lives: Michael Mallin* (Dublin: The O'Brien Press, 2012)

Kirsty Lusk and Willy Maley (eds.) *Scotland and the Easter Rising* (Edinburgh: Luath Press, 2016)

Sinead McCoole, *No Ordinary Women: Irish Female Activists in the Revolutionary Years, 1900–1923* (Dublin: The O'Brien Press, 2003)

Ruth Taillon, *The Women of 1916: When History Was Made* (Dublin: Beyond the Pale Publications, 1996)

Margaret Ward, *Unmanageable Revolutionaries: Women and Irish Nationalism* (London: Pluto Press, 1995)

Margaret Ward (ed), *In Their Own Voice: Women and Irish Nationalism* (Cork: Attic Press, 2001)

Some other books published by **Luath Press**

Scotland and the Easter Rising: Fresh Perspectives on 1916

Edited by Willy Maley and Kirsty Lusk
Afterword by Owen Dudley Edwards
ISBN 978-1-910745-36-6 PBK £12.99

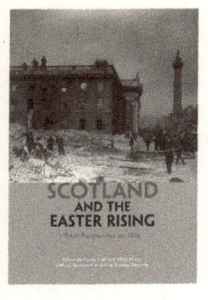

On Easter Monday 1916, leaders of a rebellion against British rule over Ireland proclaimed the establishment of an Irish Republic. Lasting only six days before surrender to the British, this event nevertheless laid the foundations for Ireland's violent path to Independence.

James Connolly and Margaret Skinnider were two Scots who played key roles in the Rising. Their stories are among the Scottish connections examined in *Scotland and the Easter Rising*, a groundbreaking collection of essays that illuminate the Scottish dimension.

Scotland and the Easter Rising is a worthy and rich book. IRISH TIMES

The Unbroken Tradition or The Irish Rebellion of 1916: A First-hand Account of the Easter Rising

Nora Connolly
ISBN: 978-1-910745-49-6 HBK £12.99

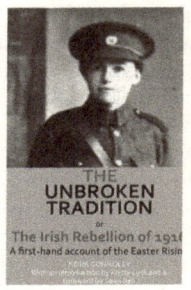

Initially banned when she tried to publish it in 1917, Nora Connolly's memoir of the Easter Rising, *The Unbroken Tradition*, was first published in the USA in 1918.

From a young age, Connolly shared the Republican and Socialist visions of her father, James Connolly. She attended meetings and lectures with him which served to deepen her sympathy with the idea of Irish independence. She was at the heart of the rebellion that aimed to free Ireland. In *The Unbroken Tradition* she offers a vivid description of Ireland in 1916 and of what it meant to be Irish and under British rule.

Details of these and other books published by Luath Press can be found at
www.luath.co.uk

Luath Press Limited

committed to publishing well written books worth reading

LUATH PRESS takes its name from Robert Burns, whose little collie Luath (*Gael.*, swift or nimble) tripped up Jean Armour at a wedding and gave him the chance to speak to the woman who was to be his wife and the abiding love of his life. Burns called one of the 'Twa Dogs' Luath after Cuchullin's hunting dog in Ossian's *Fingal*. Luath Press was established in 1981 in the heart of Burns country, and is now based a few steps up the road from Burns' first lodgings on Edinburgh's Royal Mile. Luath offers you distinctive writing with a hint of unexpected pleasures.

Most bookshops in the UK, the US, Canada, Australia, New Zealand and parts of Europe, either carry our books in stock or can order them for you. To order direct from us, please send a £sterling cheque, postal order, international money order or your credit card details (number, address of cardholder and expiry date) to us at the address below. Please add post and packing as follows: UK – £1.00 per delivery address; overseas surface mail – £2.50 per delivery address; overseas airmail – £3.50 for the first book to each delivery address, plus £1.00 for each additional book by airmail to the same address. If your order is a gift, we will happily enclose your card or message at no extra charge.

Luath Press Limited
543/2 Castlehill
The Royal Mile
Edinburgh EH1 2ND
Scotland
Telephone: +44 (0)131 225 4326 (24 hours)
Email: sales@luath.co.uk
Website: www.luath.co.uk

168